THE BOOK OF
VEGANISH

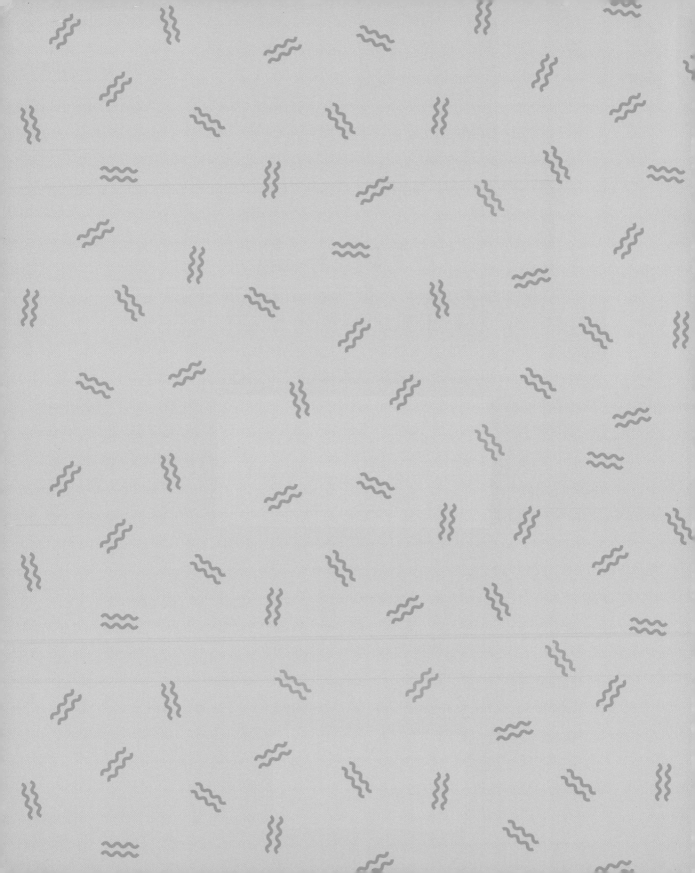

THE BOOK OF
VEGANISH

The Ultimate Guide to Easing into
a Plant-Based, Cruelty-Free,
Awesomely Delicious Way to Eat,
with 70 Easy Recipes Anyone Can Make

KATHY FRESTON
with Rachel Cohn

PAM KRAUSS BOOKS · AVERY

New York

PAM KRAUSS BOOKS | AVERY
an imprint of Penguin Random House LLC
375 Hudson Street
New York, New York 10014

Illustration on page 121 courtesy of Mercy for Animals

Most Avery books are available at special quantity discounts for bulk purchase for sales promotions, premiums, fund-raising, and educational needs. Special books or book excerpts also can be created to fit specific needs. For details, write SpecialMarkets@penguinrandomhouse.com.

Library of Congress Cataloging-in-Publication Data
Names: Freston, Kathy, author. | Cohn, Rachel, author.
Title: The book of veganish / Kathy Freston with Rachel Cohn.
Description: First edition. | New York : Pam Krauss Books, [2016] |
Audience:
Grade 9-12.? | Audience: Age 16-20.? | Includes index.
Identifiers: LCCN 2015043449 (print) | LCCN 2015051455 (ebook) | ISBN
9780553448023 | ISBN 9780553448030 | ISBN 9780553448030 ()
Subjects: LCSH: Veganism—Popular works. | Vegetarianism—Popular works.
Vegetarian cooking. | LCGFT: Cookbooks.
Classification: LCC TX392 .F8198 2016 (print) | LCC TX392 (ebook) | DDC
641.5/636—dc23
LC record available at http://lccn.loc.gov/2015043449

ISBN 9780553448023

Printed in the United States of America
1 3 5 7 9 10 8 6 4 2

BOOK DESIGN BY LAUREN KOLM AND MEIGHAN CAVANAUGH

TO YOU:

I LOVE YOU FOR BEING

CURIOUS AND CARING

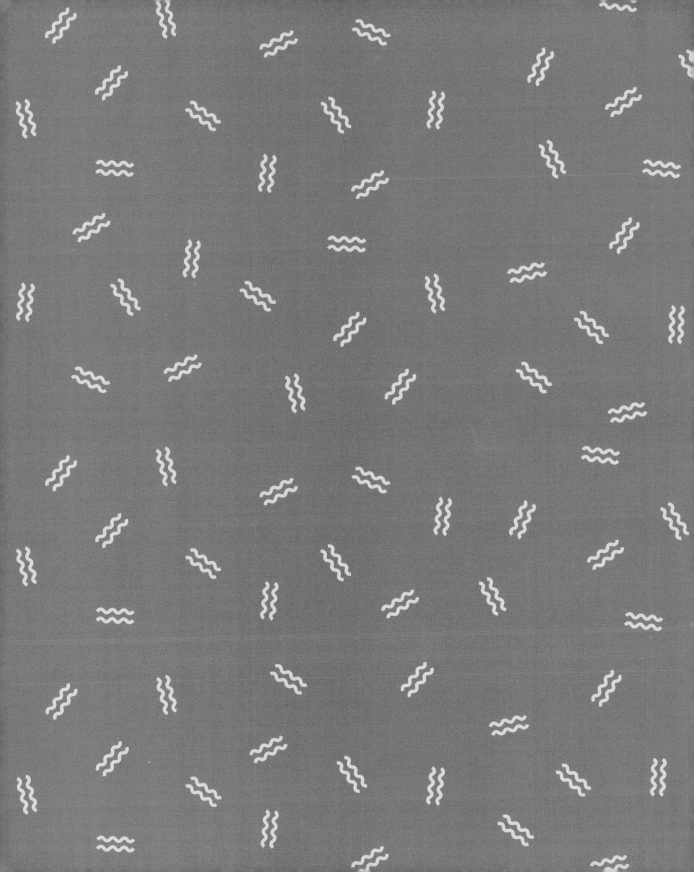

CONTENTS

1

WHAT IS VEGANISH?

So you've heard the word "vegan" and you're curious. You want to know more. Great! Welcome to the revolution that's all about living the sweet life—a way of eating that will have you looking sexy and feeling healthy while showing the world you care about the environment and animal life.

"Vegan" can be an umbrella word for a lifestyle that's thoughtful, one that looks at how our choices roll out and affect the world we live in. But I'm really not into labels. It seems like assigning labels and identifying ourselves or other people as this or that generally does more bad than good. Announcing "I'm vegan and you're a carnivore" makes people feel defensive, and it leaves no wiggle room for figuring out what feels right and true, which is always a gradual process.

Actually, it's not all black and white. The word *vegan* means different things to different people. For some, it means eliminating meat, dairy, and eggs from their diet. For others, it extends to the use of any and *all* animal products, including leather and wool. Because of that ambiguity, I like the idea of being vegan*ish* because it allows for flexibility. Veganish implies that transitioning away from animal products is important to you, but it's not a label to narrowly or exclusively define you. Veganish says: It makes sense to try and align the food I eat with my values. I do what I can and strive to be my best every single day—even if it's easier some days than others. I do things in my own time, in my own way, but I'm always pushing to do better.

Think about it: Every time you sit down to eat or dig into your wallet, you're making a choice that has a ripple effect. When you pay your tab, you're essentially saying, "I've chosen this food and I support whatever went into making it. I support it so much that I give my hard-earned money to it!" When you spend, I want you to make meaningful choices that feel good to you, rather than be a pawn to Big Food—the corporate industry of food. Big Food cares about only one thing, and it's not your well-being, or doing what's right for the land or water supply or any of the creatures that live on this earth. They only care about making a profit. They may have slick advertising that makes it look otherwise, but their bottom line *is* the bottom line.

My body is my temple, and I want to treat it righteously. It thanks me every day. —Hiro, Los Angeles, CA

If you want to make buying choices you can be proud of, if you want to show Big Food how much you care, transitioning to a plant-based diet is one of the most impactful shifts you could ever make. Moving away from animal foods is a game changer, and you can do it simply, affordably, and at your own pace. Opting for plant-based food is about navigating away from a tired, out-dated way of eating that's making a mess of our planet and causing serious worldwide health problems like obesity, heart disease, diabetes, and cancer. It's about eating mindfully, in a way that boosts your personal health and energy, and says no to destroying more of our natural resources; and it provides a more peaceful way of consuming food by not eating animals who are treated in ways that would make your stomach turn if you saw what really goes on at meat processing centers.

Do it in a way that makes you happy. Living a life of kindness also means being kind to yourself. —Emily, Los Angeles, CA

I'm sure you've looked around and noticed how many people are struggling with weight issues and the health problems that come along with obesity. You're probably aware of the monster storms and droughts and floods brought on by climate change (animal agriculture is a prime contributor to global warming, more than all fossil fuel forms of transportation—*combined*!). You may have heard about water and food being contaminated and spreading illness. Maybe you've seen a news clip of slaughterhouse workers horrifically abusing a terrified cow or chicken.

You are not naive; you know that the way our food system works—and the way both the animals and the humans involved in that system are treated—is not okay. You feel the call to do things better than those who have gone before us. (I do, too.) That awareness spreading from one person to the next will help turn the tide, both for us as individuals, and for our planet.

After air and water, food is our most primal need. We eat multiple times throughout the day, giving rhythm and order to our lives. Food literally shapes us and determines who we become. Several times a day, we decide what's okay and how highly we value our own health and well-being. After all, every bite we take ultimately works its way into the very cells and fibers of our being, and fills us up with whatever went into the making of that food. If our food choices are in sync with what we believe in—like causing no suffering or preserving nature or putting only good stuff in our bodies—then we're truly living with integrity.

I believe we absorb the frequency of what goes into our meals. Like, if I'm eating a hot dog and fries and slurp it down with a milk shake followed by a piece of cake, I'm saying it's okay that a pig was raised in extremely close quarters and strung up by her hooves for slaughter. I'm saying it's okay that a lovely mama cow was hooked up to a milking machine her whole life until she was so spent and weak after a lifetime of giving her milk that she was finally dragged off to become hamburger meat. It's okay that the hen who laid the egg that made my cake rise had her beak and toes seared off so she wouldn't peck at her peers from the sheer madness of being locked up. I'm saying okay to the fat storing itself in my cells and some Big Food company hooking me in with addictive sugars and dangerous chemicals. I'm saying okay to the toll on human workers in slaughterhouses who are exposed to horrific workplace environments and unhealthy levels of ammonia and pathogens. I'm saying, "Yeah, I'll go for that. I'll take that in and let it settle into my body."

I think since I've become vegan I appreciate everything more. It opened my eyes to all the cruelty involved in making things humans want. It also awakened something inside me that makes me want to speak up about things I believe in, like veganism, feminism, LGBT rights, etc. Veganism has turned me into an activist. —Cianna, Whittier, CA

Personally, I don't *want* to go for food that makes me feel dead instead of alive. I want to love myself and put positivity out into the world. I honor and respect myself enough to only invite in the good. I want to be part of the solution, not the problem. I am nobody's fool, and I won't play into some deceptive corporate strategy for profiting off what they know is addictive and harmful. I am a player in life, and I will not *be played*. I'm awake and aware and I am taking steps (and bites!) toward my best self.

That message feels empowering, nourishing. I feel like I can do anything when my fuel is so positive. And I want you to feel that way, too.

Don't get me wrong: I love comfort foods. I like burgers and pizza and chili. I love hanging with my friends and family, and I really love having fun. I want order in my life but not the drag of strict, inflexible discipline. I want it all, but I want it in a way that sits well with me when I consider it from all angles. If that rings true for you, too, I'm here to offer a little guidance along your way.

To be super clear: There are no rules to going veganish. There's no hard and fast way one "should" be. This book is *not* about limiting your diet to a plate of vegetables (how boring!), or starving yourself by subscribing to a rigid belief system. No way. It's about figuring out what's important to you, what you value and what you won't tolerate or be a part of, and then taking action on your beliefs through tasty, hearty, and healthy food.

> *Veganism's made me feel a hell of a lot more optimistic about a bunch of things. It's a lifestyle that can address drought, save the lives of animals, encourage more ethical shifts in massive agribusiness, mitigate global climate change, and do so much more. —Julie, San Francisco, CA*

Wherever you are now—from full-on carnivore to part-time vegetarian—this book will give you tools for translating your value system into an entirely, or mostly, animal-free diet. You don't have to do everything perfectly and you don't have to do it all at once. You know what's right and what's wrong, and I'm here with tools and tips to help you move toward what feels right for you.

Bonus: *It doesn't have to be hard.* It's about setting an intention, and then gently nudging yourself in that direction. I love what the nineteenth-century French writer Victor Hugo said: "Perfection is the enemy of the good." That makes sense to me. We tend not to stick with things if they're too hard or punishing. We need to find our way gradually and become familiar with a new way of being over time. My advice is to ditch the pressure that comes along with trying to be perfect from the jump. You'll get there if it's important to you. I'll help you figure out the "hows."

It took me a long time to give up animal products, and I did it very gradually. I've become a big believer in "progress, not perfection." Rather than a full-on, all-or-nothing leap, I recommend you start with small steps. "Swap out" rather than "cut out," feels more doable, right? Start by observing Meatless Mondays, or substituting meat burgers or meatballs with alternatives like veggie burgers or meatless meatballs. Instead of that beef burrito or chicken enchilada, try a black bean burrito; add some guacamole and salsa, and maybe substitute a cashew or soy cheese for dairy cheese. These are all delicious and satisfying meals—more so I think you'll find, because you're aligning your taste with your conscience.

While some people can go cold turkey—and good for them!—most of us can't go veg overnight. I firmly believe it's better to go some of the way than no way at all. Partway vegan—veganish—*absolutely counts*. And not only does it count, but it's more likely to stick.

The payoff is huge. Your body will reward you over time. Get ready: Your skin is going to get clear and bright, and your energy is going to skyrocket. You are going to feel stronger and more energetic than you've ever felt before, and there's going to be a light in your eyes that people will comment on. (It's true! You'll see!) You're going to feel a happiness you've not yet experienced, and you're going to sense a profound connection to life itself. Research shows irrefutably that people who don't eat a lot of (or any) animal foods live longer and better lives. Eliminating meat leads naturally, even effortlessly, to weight loss and blood sugar balancing (because plant-based foods are naturally rich in fiber, which slows down the release of blood sugar and metabolizes food in a steady way), and can even reverse or halt serious illnesses like heart disease and cancer. (A deeper dive on all of this later.)

The benefits don't stop there. Going veganish is one of the most direct and effective ways to make a difference in the world. While it's unrealistic to think that your personal choices can cause the global population to suddenly stop consuming animal products, the truth is that *your actions actually do make a huge difference.*

As you progress on your path toward becoming veganish or even fully vegan, you're going to hear a lot of conflicting information about what you do or don't need in your diet, sometimes from people who love and care for you. Naysayers will quote research that supports eating meat and dairy products like milk and eggs. You'll hear about meat-heavy diets

When I made the transition to being vegan, I noticed a major difference in my eating habits and physical and emotional well-being. I was constantly eating, but I began to lose weight. My diet was now so high in fiber, protein, and good fat that I noticed my body became leaner and less cellulite was on my legs and backside. Emotionally, I was a lot happier. I've struggled with body image issues my whole life and it wasn't until I became vegan that these issues were put aside and I could live my life. I went from counting calories and trying fad diets to eating whenever I wanted and having more energy. I used to be in a constant battle with food, but now I love food and have a great relationship with my refrigerator. —Christina, Boca Raton, FL

like Atkins and Paleo. Your own doctor may express concern that you'll be cheating yourself out of nutrients you need. You're going to get confused. (Who wouldn't?) So let me assure you that the veganish diet has stood the test of time (since Plato and Aristotle, two of the original supporters of meat-free eating!), and it's an extremely healthy way to eat. I can tell you with absolute certainty that the research supporting plant-based diets is plentiful and credible, and I'll go into that more throughout the rest of this book.

But if your intention wavers in the face of someone insisting you need "animal protein" for whatever reason, focus on the ethical piece of a plant-based diet. Let your heart guide you, and you'll know what's right. When you feel the personal effect and how big it is, nothing will be able to sway you, no matter how much you're bombarded with (mis)information. Act with your integrity, and nothing will stop you.

You're right on time—actually, you're just out ahead of the curve. You're going to look back on this shift and be so proud that you were part of it. Seriously, this movement is righteous.

WHY GO VEGANISH?

Top Five Reasons to Go Veganish

Let me tell you what you'll get out of this mission you're looking into. (Spoiler alert: It's all *so* good!)

1. You will say no to trashing precious natural resources, like water, the rain forests, and fresh, clean air. That's because so much of animal agriculture wrecks nature. Depleted rain forests and cesspools of poop and greenhouse gasses are just some of the major harms caused by animal agriculture.
2. You'll be on an easy and natural path to ideal weight, clear skin, soaring energy, balanced blood sugar, and the prevention of some serious health problems.
3. You won't be contributing to animal suffering. 'Nuf said.
4. You'll be happier. People who eat plant-based foods have far less depression, anxiety, and other mood problems. Maybe it's as simple as how alive and purposeful we feel when we know we're making a positive difference in the world?
5. You'll eat well without breaking the bank. Animal foods are expensive, go bad quickly, and cost taxpayers a whole lot of money in both agricultural subsidies, healthcare costs, and fixing the damage climate change causes.

There are *so many* great reasons to move toward an animal-free diet!

ETHICS

I hold that the more helpless a creature, the more entitled it is to protection by man from the cruelty of man.

—GANDHI

MY JOURNEY

Here's how it started for me: One day I was playing with my little dog Lhotse. I was rubbing her belly and loving her up and thinking that she was one of the greatest joys of my life. She was wagging her tail and I swear she was smiling from the attention. I thought, *I love this dog so much! Animals are just pure love. They aren't manipulative or mean or spiteful. They are just simple innocent creatures.* And then a little voice inside of me asked, "Well . . . if you think animals are so lovely, why do you eat them? Because you know that animal went through sheer hell to end up on your plate." I thought: *Because it's a habit. Because I like the taste of meat.*

> *I love animals. My mom's uncle owned a dairy farm and I used to love letting the calves suck on my fingers. One night, my family was eating at a fancy restaurant and I ordered veal, not knowing what it was. My dad explained that veal was baby cow and I stopped eating meat right then. —Jessica, Sandpoint, ID*

Then I started picturing my dog as one of those food animals, locked up in a tiny cage like a chicken or a pig for her whole (short, horrible) life, and then being flung onto a truck and driven to the slaughterhouse to be killed. I knew my dog, and I knew that she had this wide range of senses and emotions, and that if she were crammed into a slaughterhouse with all those awful smells and sounds of death, she'd be terrified. Shaking, eyes wide, flat-out terrified. I, of course, would do anything to save my dog from a fate like that, anything to keep her from that sort of trauma and suffering. I mean, I hated to even leave her alone for a few hours, so this connection was blowing my mind.

A lightbulb went on, right then and there. I felt it to my core. Suddenly I realized that the

only difference between my dog and the cow or chicken or pig that ended up on my plate was that I knew my dog. I knew her personality and quirks and traits; I knew when she was worried or sad or excited or wanted to go for a walk. Lhotse was an individual to me, not a something. If I were to get to know those other animals in the slaughterhouse as individuals outside of that live-stock horror house, I knew they'd be as endearing and lovable as she was.

> Don't focus on perfection, or some vegans saying you're not "vegan enough" because you do this or that. To me, being veganish is simply about doing your best to cause the least amount of harm. —Sarah, Portland, OR

I remembered what Charles Darwin, who studied animals and humans from every biological perspective, taught us: There is no fundamental difference between man and animals in their ability to feel pleasure and pain, happiness and misery. Recent science has shown what dog and cat lovers have always known: that animals can anticipate the future, delay gratification, dream, play, use language and tools, and are more like us than unlike us.

Gulp. I was beginning to understand that if I bought or ordered meat, dairy, or eggs, I was playing a part in causing a thinking, feeling, vulnerable creature to suffer unthinkable misery, much like the misery I myself would experience if I were locked up in the dark until I grew big enough to kill, and then did the death march to my violent end. It became starkly simple for me: I had to ask myself, Can I look right into the eyes of a scared animal and say, "I really don't care that you're hurting and terrified and you're about to be strung up and slaughtered; I have a craving for one of your body parts slathered in sauce or fried up and put between two slices of bread."

> The biggest factor for giving up animal foods for me was that I was decreasing the quality of life for so many animals when I didn't need to. I just thought about how ridiculous it was that animals had to be confined and killed just so I could have bacon-wrapped everything. It was cruel and unjust, and something I wouldn't want done to me, so why do it to someone else? —Nick, Gainesville, FL

Besides the way they look, there's no difference between Lhotse and a pig. Or chicken. Or cow. They all feel pain, and struggle to live. They are not unaware of cruel treatment. They do experience fear and dread. I decided I didn't want to participate in that kind of suffering. My body felt better and stronger for that choice, but more important, so did my heart and soul.

A MATTER OF JUSTICE

You may or may not have that personal connection with animals, but I think that ethical eating is also a matter of social justice: All beings deserve equal consideration based on their needs. Cats don't need the right to vote and dogs don't need to drive, but they both deserve to live in a loving home free from abuse. Pigs deserve their families, birds deserve to fly, and orcas deserve to swim. Not equal rights, but equal consideration. There is no argument that justifies our current treatment of animals. No just argument. No ethical argument. Might does not make right.

There are so many great resources for investigating this topic; so many brave and inspiring people on the front lines who are helping to expose what really happens in slaughterhouses or on a farm where concentrated animal feeding practices are observed. These people are my biggest heroes, because to experience what they do—the squirming terror of a

> *I love knowing that I am being honest with myself and not contributing to an industry that is harming living beings who have every right to live on this planet peacefully.*
> —*Dana, East Brunswick, NJ*

cow who smells death and doesn't want to die or a chicken who is dunked alive, upside down into scalding water or a pig who is strung up by her hooves as she is mechanically moved toward the blade that will dismember her—all in the name of getting the truth out there, well, that's just a trauma I could not endure. Since these undercover investigators give their lives to this work, I figure I have a responsibility at the very least to watch the videos or read the accounts they post. It's effing grueling. Really opening my eyes to the truth of what happens to food animals is the hardest thing I have ever done or will do, but it's nothing compared to what animals endure for their entire lives.

A snippet of these docs is enough to make me think, *That's the old way of doing things. I don't want to be a part of supporting that system or those practices.* I'm all about moving forward, especially when there are so many delicious, nourishing foods I can eat that don't come from an animal. It's incredibly selfish of me to think animals were put on earth simply to satisfy my appetite. That they suffer so badly and experience so much fear just makes it that much harder to justify.

So, if we start taking little bits of information, watch a minute or two of a video, read an article, then little by little, we are able to take in the enormity of what's going on and denial is chipped away. Thousands of years of culture that condones eating animals will take a long time to dismantle, but each time we look—*really look*—at what happens to animals, we take a positive step toward ending their suffering. As Albert Einstein (himself a vegetarian) famously said, "The world is a dangerous place, not because of those who do evil but because of those who look on and do nothing."

To learn more, go to the websites for Mercy for Animals, PETA2, Farm Sanctuary, or Humane Society of the United States. Scan their videos (my top choices are PETA's "Glass Walls," Mercy for Animals' "Farm to Fridge," and Farm Sanctuary's "What Came Before"). Or Google "slaughterhouse meat" and/or "factory farming." Watch the documentaries *Earthlings* and *Food, Inc.* Take in as much as you can. Know that these horrific reports reflect industry-wide practices, not the actions of isolated, sadistic producers. Most of what you see are the everyday, legal methods of raising and killing the animals we eat. Or ate . . . before our eyes opened.

> When you go vegan, the only thing you give up is cruelty! Cutting a large part of your diet out may seem scary, but instead of focusing on what you are giving up, embrace all of the new, exciting, and delicious foods you will be replacing them with. —Lia, Romeoville, IL

VEGANISH = HAPPINESS!

It's actually pretty simple. There's a body-mind connection when you eat wholesome plant-based foods. You have so much more energy, and you're feeling stronger, leaner, and cleaner. And when your body feels and looks great, your mood soars right along with it.

You feel like you can do anything, because you have the energy to do it. All those antioxidants you get in the colorful fruits and vegetables make your immune system superstrong, so you get sick a whole lot less. How much happier do you think you'll be by not going to the doctor, missing class/work, or paying for expensive pharmaceuticals? A lot, trust me!

It's not fun battling the bulge or dealing with bad skin. When you don't look good, you don't feel good about yourself. When you feed yourself food that's colorful and

> Veganism has changed my life forever. Before I was vegan, I thought on an individual point of view. I did not consider how my actions affected others, humans and animals alike. After going veg, I began to consider how my actions affected others, and what I can do to prevent as much unnecessary suffering as possible. —Kadedra, Norfolk, VA

> *My ninety-year-old grandmother lives in Queens, and she has lived in New York all her life. On one of my most recent visits, she and I were waiting for the elevator in her apartment building. We had just had a lovely meal in the building's café, and she was asking me about veganism after noticing that I had requested no cheese in my salad. I answered her questions, and then she said something amazing: "You know, ever since you started this thing, I've stopped eating so much meat. I guess I've started to see a face with my food." This, to me, is still one of the most remarkable statements I ever heard regarding transitions in diet. If a ninety-year-old Jewish New Yorker with a taste for beef and gefilte fish can change, anybody can!* —Lydia, New York, NY

chock-full of vitamins and nutrients while avoiding dull, colorless flesh foods, you see those good choices show up in clearer skin and a leaner body.

Just as important? *Practicing kindness makes you feel good.* When you perform a good deed or an act of kindness, your mood gets a nice bump. Knowing you didn't cause pain or suffering by the foods you choose to eat is an easy "act of kindness" you can perform three times a day. And not only is it a quick boost, researchers at Harvard and the University of British Columbia showed in a study that was published in the *Journal of Happiness Studies* that performing these little acts of kindness has a much longer and more profound effect on your overall sense of well-being and long-term happiness. By expressing kindness, you begin to see yourself as "a good person," and that affects your self-esteem and outlook on life. When you feel like you're doing good things in the world (i.e., not eating animals), you feel like you deserve goodness looping back to you. Kind of like you're setting your own good karma!

Having a sense of belonging or being part of a community generally makes us happier and more peaceful, right? Well, there are some really good people who are excited about changing the world through bettering their food choices, and it feels so exhilarating to be part of that movement. Knowing that you're out front in making positive changes in the world—both for human health and for the well-being of animals—feels *so good.*

HEALTH

Your good health depends on having a superstrong immune system.

We've known for a long time that the immune function of non-meat eaters may be more effective than that of meat eaters. Researchers at the German Cancer Research Center published a report in 1989 that found that although vegetarians had the same number of disease-fighting white blood cells compared to meat eaters, the immune cells of vegetarians were twice as effective in destroying their targets—not only cancer cells, but virus-infected cells as well. The message is clear: When you eat your fruits and veggies, and avoid animal foods, your body thrives.

ZONE IN ON WHAT WORKS

Have you heard about the Blue Zones? They are the five places in the world where people have historically lived the longest and are the healthiest. *National Geographic* explorer Dan Buettner spent over a decade researching how and why people remained strong and relatively disease-free in some areas of the world, while in most other areas people tended to get fat and sick much earlier on in their lives. You might assume people in the most modern cultures would be most likely to thrive, but that's actually not the case.

Dan found that in each of these five places—Okinawa, Japan; the Highlands of Sardinia, Italy; Ikaria, Greece; the Nicoya Peninsula of Costa Rica; and Loma Linda, California—there were certain shared ways of living. In each of the five Blue Zones, people ate a primarily plant-based diet, and not because they were opposed to eating animals (with the exception of the Seventh-day Adventists of Loma Linda, California, who believe the Bible

Since going vegan, I have felt incredible! As soon as I ditched dairy from my diet, I lost a healthy amount of weight and my skin cleared up almost immediately. Also, I am no longer anemic and I haven't been constipated in months! Additionally, going vegan has had such a tremendous effect on my mental health. Ever since I changed my diet, I have not experienced nearly as much depression or anxiety as I did prior to the transition. I feel more energetic during the day and am able to sleep through the night for the first time in memory! —Lydia, New York, NY

encourages a vegetarian or vegan diet). They ate that way because animal foods were more expensive and scarce, so their diets focused on potatoes, grains, vegetables, nuts, fruits, and, above all, beans.

People in these places were largely isolated, living either way up in the hills or on an island. Meat was typically hard to come by, especially during times of war and hardship when they had to "endure" a very simple, humble diet of foods they could grow and gather from the land directly around them. These were essentially simple folks—not wealthy, and very hard-working. (The Adventists are the exception, as they do enjoy a good bit of wealth, as do many of the newly deemed Blue Zones that Dan has helped establish.) They were strong enough to work the land and tend to their homes way into their *nineties* (can you imagine that today?), with a surprising number of them living past the age of 100.

"Modern" foods were not part of their diets. They didn't have burger joints or pizza parlors or soda. Cow's milk was nearly nonexistent. They had meat maybe once or twice a week, and even then it was just a small bit, often as part of a celebration or a special meal. And they *thrived*. They weren't counting calories or trying to build muscle or stay lean or live a long and healthy life; they never thought about any of those things. Those benefits just *happened* to them. Granted, there were other lifestyle factors that played a part, such as having strong family ties, lifelong friends, and a tight community, but diet was the foundational starting point. The Blue Zones research team isn't sure if they enjoyed this wellness because they ate so much healthy fiber (which is only found in plant foods) or because they got so many nutrients from local fruits and vegetables or because they ate very little meat, but the end result was very long, healthy lives.

What's interesting to note is that once these populations started to enjoy more wealth and access to "modern" foods, their long-held trend of health and longevity ended. As people could afford to eat more animal foods, they began gaining weight and getting sicker younger. A diet of mostly plant-based foods had seemed to keep people strong, but as meat, dairy, and processed foods became more prominent in their diets, they started to slide in terms of health. In fact, people in the Blue Zones (again, with the exception of the Loma Linda Adventists) born roughly after the year 1946 could no longer count on the long lives their ancestors had historically enjoyed.

Eating as much meat and other animal foods as we do is actually a pretty recent development. Although the Paleo diet supporters would have you believe that ancient humans ate animal foods every day (and three times a day, at that!), it just isn't true. It took a lot of work to hunt down and kill an animal, and paleontologists think it's much more likely that our ancestors were foraging vegetarians who didn't turn down the occasional carcass when they found one. Robert Dunn writes in *Scientific American*, "What do other living primates, the ones with guts mostly like ours, eat? The diets of nearly all monkeys and apes (except the leaf-eaters) are composed of fruits, nuts, leaves, insects, and sometimes the odd snack of a bird or a lizard. Meat is a rare treat, if eaten at all. The job of a generalist primate gut is primarily to eat pieces of plants."

When we were hunters and gatherers, scarcity of food was the problem, which is why the concentrated fat, calories, and protein in meat were beneficial for early humans, who were desperate for calories. Today, we have access to a huge variety of food and getting enough calories is not an issue in our developed world. Although the occasional bit of animal food might have sustained our hungry ancestors, today we don't need it. In fact, we're better off without it.

> *My blood pressure and cholesterol are lower than they've ever been, and my skin is clearer. My teeth seem to have gotten whiter after going vegan! I also feel emotionally healthier. I think that since my eating choices now align with my values, I just feel more at peace.* —Sarah, Bloomington, IN

WE NEED FIBER, FIBER, FIBER!

Animal foods have no fiber. Unprocessed plant foods, like grains or beans or potatoes or veggies, are chock-full of it. Fiber is the scrub brush that pushes crap through your body (and I mean that both literally and figuratively). The human intestine is long and windy with little notches along the way. If you're not eating plenty of fiber, that crap gets stuck in those notches and it putrefies, becoming toxic over time. And you get constipated and big-bellied.

But fiber does more than just help move the digestive process along. Fiber feeds the good bacteria in your gut that keep your immune system healthy and help you extract nutrients from the food you eat. It also fills you up so that you feel satiated and don't overeat. It takes about a quart of food to fill up the typical stomach. If that quart were made up of calories from meat and/or dairy foods, you'd have to ingest over 5,000 calories to feel satisfied, which is way more than you need (or should get) in a day. If you're eating plant foods, their fiber fills you up faster. When you feel satiated, you don't overeat. The other great thing about fiber is that it helps keep your blood sugar in the normal range because it allows your food to be digested and absorbed into your bloodstream slowly.

> Plant foods give you fiber.
> Animal foods do not. Zilch, nada, none.

WHAT DO WE NOT NEED?

Animal foods don't have fiber, but they do have a lot of saturated fat and cholesterol. Here's what the National Institutes of Health says about cholesterol on their website:

Your blood cholesterol level has a lot to do with your chances of getting heart disease. High blood cholesterol is one of the major risk factors for heart disease. A risk factor is a condition that increases your chance of getting a disease. In fact, the higher your blood cholesterol level, the greater your risk for developing heart disease or having a heart attack. Heart disease is the number one killer of women and men in the United States. Each year, more than a million Americans have heart attacks, and about a half million people die from heart disease.

How Does Cholesterol Cause Heart Disease?

When there is too much cholesterol (a fat-like substance) in your blood, it builds up in the walls of your arteries. Over time, this buildup causes "hardening of the arteries" so that arteries become narrowed and blood flow to the heart is slowed down or blocked. The blood carries oxygen to the heart, and if enough blood and oxygen cannot reach your heart, you may suffer chest pain. If the blood supply to a portion of the heart is completely cut off by a blockage, the result is a heart attack.

High blood cholesterol itself does not cause symptoms, so many people are unaware that their cholesterol level is too high. It is important to find out what your cholesterol numbers are because lowering cholesterol levels that are too high lessens the risk for developing heart disease and reduces the chance of a heart attack or dying of heart disease, even if you already have it. Cholesterol lowering is important for everyone—younger, middle age, and older adults; women and men; and people with or without heart disease.

Guess what has no cholesterol? Yep—plant-based food! Animals, not plants, produce cholesterol, which is why when we eat animal foods, we eat a lot of cholesterol. Our bodies produce all the cholesterol we need; we do not need the extra dietary cholesterol found in meat, dairy, or eggs.

Now, if you bring up the cholesterol issue to your pro-meat friends, they are likely to say, "The dietary cholesterol thing has been disputed, and eating foods with high cholesterol—like meat or dairy or eggs—doesn't affect your blood cholesterol. That's what the studies are showing. When people eat dietary cholesterol in eggs or meat, their blood cholesterol number doesn't go up."

I've consulted with the fine folks at the Physician's Committee for Responsible Medicine, and their doctors explained to me why the (animal-agriculture industry-funded) studies are showing that: When there is a raging fire and you throw a lit match into it, there is no detectable difference in the fire. That's why people who already eat a lot of animal foods and have high cholesterol don't show a bump when they eat more animal foods. Their "fire" is already raging. But give that animal food to a vegan, and the cholesterol shoots up. That's the real effect of the "lit match"—it bumps up the blood cholesterol count.

And what about cholesterol's cousin, saturated fat? This is how the Mayo Clinic describes it on their website, and the news is not good:

Saturated fat is a type of fat that comes mainly from animal sources of food, such as red meat, poultry and full-fat dairy products. Saturated fat raises total blood cholesterol levels and low-density lipoprotein (LDL) cholesterol levels, which can increase your risk of cardiovascular disease. Saturated fat may also increase your risk of type 2 diabetes.

THE C-WORD

Now let's talk cancer. It might feel like that's not something to worry about at this stage in your life, but with every bite of food, you're influencing your body to go one way or the other. Let's talk about it now, so you can move on to feeling great.

> I've lost over 70 pounds, despite always being a "fat kid." Going vegan really helped me to lose the final 20 or so. I'm happier and healthier than I've ever been before, and veganism helped me get there.
> —Tyler, Columbus, OH

The docs and nutritional scientists at the Physician's Committee for Responsible Medicine have this to say about the link between cancer and animal foods:

In 2007, the American Institute for Cancer Research (AICR) published their second review of the major studies on food, nutrition, and cancer prevention. For cancers of the oesophagus, lung, pancreas, stomach, collorectum, endometrium, and prostate, it was determined that red meat (beef, pork, or lamb) and processed meat consumption increased cancer risk. For colorectal cancer, a review of the literature determined that there is convincing scientific evidence that red meat increased cancer risk and that processed meat, saturated/animal fat, and heavily cooked meat were also convincing of increased risk.

A number of hypotheses have been advanced to explain the connection between meat consumption and cancer risk. First, meat is devoid of fiber and other nutrients that have a protective effect. Meat also contains animal protein, saturated fat, and, in some cases, carcinogenic compounds such as heterocyclic amines (HCA) and polycyclic aromatic hydrocarbons (PAH) formed during the processing or cooking of meat. HCAs, formed as meat is cooked at high temperatures, and PAHs, formed during the burning of organic substances, are believed to increase cancer risk. In addition, the high fat content of meat and other animal products increases hormone production, thus increasing the risk of hormone-related cancers such as breast and prostate cancer.

THE D-WORD

And since two out of every three people will be diagnosed as diabetic or pre-diabetic during their lifetime, let's explore the link between diabetes and animal foods. The more fat there is in the diet, the harder it is for insulin to get glucose into the cells, where it can be put to work. Dr. Neal Barnard, founder of PCRM and an adjunct professor of medicine at George Washington University, explains it like this:

The key is to help our body's insulin to work normally. So long as your body's insulin can escort glucose into the cells normally, diabetes will not occur. The resistance to insulin that leads to diabetes appears to be caused by a buildup of fat inside the muscle cells and also inside the liver. Let me draw an analogy: I arrive home from work one day and put my key in my front door lock. But I notice the key does not turn properly, and the door does not open. Peering inside the lock, I see that someone has jammed chewing gum into the lock. Now, if the insulin "key" cannot open up the cell to glucose, there is something interfering with it. It's not chewing gum, of course. The problem is fat. In the same way that chewing gum in a lock makes it hard to open your front door, fat particles inside muscle cells interfere with insulin's efforts to open the cell to glucose. This fat comes from beef, chicken, fish, cooking oils, dairy products, etc. The answer is to avoid these fatty foods. People who avoid all animal products obviously get no animal fat at all, they appear to have much less fat buildup inside their cells, and their risk of diabetes is extremely low.

Being vegan has made me realize that you truly are what you eat; what you put into your body fuels your body.
—Laura, Seattle, WA

POPULARITY DOES NOT EQUAL HEALTHY

Let's look at the most popularly consumed animal foods themselves, and consider why transitioning away from them is a good idea. Because I want you to have a long, healthy, happy life!

CHICKEN: Even so-called lean, white meat chicken is loaded with fat and cholesterol—one 3.5-ounce portion has about 85 milligrams cholesterol and 23 percent of its calories come from fat (bad for your heart, bad for your weight). Equally disturbing is the fact that about a third of all chicken sold is contaminated with salmonella or campylobacter, which can make you seriously sick. (That bacteria comes from the chicken's poop, which gets splattered onto the skin and muscle tissue—aka meat—during the slaughter and evisceration process.) Cooking does kill the germs, but it doesn't kill the germs that get all over your kitchen counter, cutting board, or hands as you unwrap the bird, and that can get transferred to your salad or other foods.

BEEF: There may be a worse way to get your protein and iron, but I don't know what it is. Beef is full of artery-clogging cholesterol and saturated fat, which increases your waistline and your risk of getting cancer, having a heart attack or becoming diabetic. Frightening fact: According to research cited by PCRM, beef eaters are nine times more likely to be seriously obese than vegans are. Plus, I'm sorry to put it this way, but cows are scared shitless in slaughterhouses, so they poop all over themselves and walk in it, and it's hard to keep the meat from getting contaminated. So when you eat a burger or a steak, you're often ingesting bacteria along with any antibiotics the cow may have been fed (most farmers do this to make the cows grow fatter faster and keep them alive long enough to get to slaughter weight).

FISH: You may know some people who pass on the meat but still eat the fish. Seems like a good compromise, right? At least fish are able to live most of their lives in the wild, right? Unfortunately, too many fish are raised in supercrowded pens in what amounts to "factory farms in water." The water is doused with pesticides and all kinds of chemicals because things can get pretty dirty when you cram tons of pooping, freaked-out fish into a confined space, and a lot of that gunk ends up in the flesh that we eat. Even "wild caught" fish presents a problem: When we eat fish from the sea, we're eating all the stuff they've been exposed to in our polluted oceans, including dangerous levels of mercury. Mercury is emitted into the air by industrial activity, like coal-fired electricity generation, smelting, and the incineration of waste. It settles into our oceans and waterways and then into the fish that live there. A *Wall Street Journal* story some years back told the story of a kid who went from honor student and athlete to remedial classes and being unable to catch a ball—all because he ate a lot of tuna, which was laden with mercury. So much for "Fish is brain food"!

The Office of Environmental Health Hazard Assessment warns that it's not only mercury we need to worry about, but also "PCBs, dioxins, chlordane, the DDT group, and dieldrin." Those last tongue twisters are all generated from industrial activities. That pollution is released into the environment and taken up by the fish, then eaten by unsuspecting humans. Our oceans are so polluted that it's almost impossible to avoid getting contaminated fish. Aside from that, certain fatty fish (the kind that's supposed to be good for us because of their abundance of omega-3s) is just that: fatty. There is very little omega-3 in the flesh of fish. Besides, you can get that omega-3 from flax or avocados, or by taking an algae supplement—after all, algae is where the fish get their omegas in the first place!

CHEESE: You already know that cheese is high in calories and saturated fat, which pad your body with extra weight. You may not know that cheese (like all dairy products) produces casomorphins—compounds formed in your digestive tract when

(continued)

your body is breaking down the dairy that are literally addictive. The root word *morphin* is in there because, just like morphine, dairy is habit forming, and a trigger for dangerous binge eating. Why this natural phenomenon? Because the addictiveness is an evolutionary biological impulse that keeps a baby calf close to her mama so she will keep nursing in order to grow. It's a survival mechanism. Unfortunately we humans get addicted to the fatty cheese, too, even though we don't need it for survival, and just want more and more.

MILK: Yes, it's a source of protein and calcium. But remember, milk is the bodily fluid secreted by a female mammal for the nourishment of her young. It's naturally full of estrogen. Estrogen is a growth hormone, and growth hormones can fan the flames of cancer cells and make them grow; it's been linked especially to hormone-dependent cancers, like breast and prostate. I'm not even talking about the additional hormones that some dairy producers feed to their cattle. (Dairy cows are always pregnant or have just given birth because that's the only way to keep them producing milk.) I'm talking about what's naturally occurring in cows who are constantly either pregnant or have just given birth.

There's also a dangerous hormone called insulin-like growth factor (aka IGF-1), which is a well-known culprit for fanning the flames of cancer and other inflammatory conditions like acne. But aside from the hormone issues, consider this: Cow milk was designed for a mother cow to feed her calf so it can grow to its ultimate size—about an average of *fifteen hundred* pounds—not a goal weight for humans!

EGGS: One egg has as much cholesterol as an 8-ounce steak and studies show that guys who eat more than 2.5 eggs per week increase their chances of getting prostate cancer—by more than 80 percent! Don't be fooled: The egg industry has funded research that refutes the connection between eating eggs and high blood cholesterol. But here's the thing: If you already have high cholesterol and eat eggs, the cholesterol in those eggs won't make much of a difference; you're already an unhealthy eater. Remember the raging fire analogy on page 17? But when a healthy person who doesn't have high cholesterol eats eggs, their bad cholesterol level shoots up. Because their health is not an already raging fire, that "lit match" packs a punch. And have you seen videos of those poor hens living in filthy sheds or cages pushing an egg out of their vajayjays? Yes, they are eventually cleaned and sterilized, but *gross*. (Let me interject this fun fact: One egg has only 6 grams of protein, while one cup of lentils has a whopping *18 grams* of protein. And lots of fiber. So if you're looking for protein, you're getting a better deal with beans or lentils.)

WARM HEART, HOT BODY

It's human nature to want to do the best for ourselves. And let's be honest: On a vanity level, wouldn't it be a nice bonus to look and feel great as a result of your righteous food choices?

In my experience, people who eat little or no meat or dairy are some of the most gorgeous human beings walking the planet! Musicians like Beyoncé, J-Lo, Miley Cyrus, Ariana Grande, Sia, Grimes, Travis Barker, and Shania Twain. Actors like Portia de Rossi, Daisy Fuentes, Liam Hemsworth, Ellen Page, Jared Leto, Jenna Dewan-Tatum, Lea Michele, Jessica Chastain, Maggie Q, and Alicia Silverstone; athletes like NFL running back David Carter, Ultimate Fighting Championship winner Mac Danzig, triathlete and ultra-marathoner Rich Roll, NFL star Ricky Williams, champion triathelete and Ironman Brendan Brazier, "Olympian of the Century" Carl Lewis, and, of course, talk show host and comedienne Ellen DeGeneres. These are seriously strong and charismatic people, and some of the world's most successful. There's a light in their eyes and fierceness about what they do.

There's no magic pill to get their kind of fit body and glowing skin—the not-so-secret method is to eat nutrient-dense, fiber-filled foods, stay hydrated, and exercise. It really is that simple.

NATURAL WEIGHT CONTROL

Walk into any vegan restaurant and you probably won't see many people there who are overweight. While it's absolutely possible to be vegan and overweight (if you over-consume and/or subsist on junk food), chunky vegans are the exception rather than the rule. That's because plant-based staples like beans, grains, fruits, and vegetables are fiber-rich and naturally lean, and don't contain the fatty animal stuff that leads to weight gain and bad skin. Instead, plant foods fill you up and make you lean. And if you're someone who works out a lot, you'll recover faster and have more energy to train hard. (Fun fact: Some of the fittest humans eat veganish food, and so do many of the natural world's strongest and most powerful animals: stallions, bulls, and gorillas, for instance!)

> *I felt a palpable weight lift off my shoulders, a weight I didn't even know was there. I felt lighter emotionally, too. The world seemed happier. My depression and PTSD receded enormously. I'd always been thin, but also always have had stubborn belly fat. It's no longer stubborn. I've noticed it's easier for me to gain muscle, too—finally! —Joshua, Seattle, WA*

> *Veganism brought me out of the depths of an eating disorder. When I became vegan, I made diet choices based on things well beyond myself. What I was doing was making a real difference. This was new and it helped me to stop counting calories and start counting good deeds. —Brianna, Philadelphia, PA*

Unlike animal foods, which pack more calories ounce for ounce (which is why they are called *calorie*-dense), *nutrient*-dense plant-based food is ideal for maintaining a lean, healthy weight. Here's why:

- Meat and dairy are concentrated sources of fat and calories. Fat and calories make you fat. Period.
- Animal foods have no fiber in them at all. The one dietary component that has consistently proven beneficial in all the science across the board is *fiber*. It bears repeating: Fiber fills you up, cleans you out, lowers cholesterol, and burns calories. You can *only* find fiber in foods that are plant-based—like whole grains; beans such as chickpeas, lentils, or black beans; and of course fruits and veggies. Also, fiber foods are probiotic and feed the good bacteria in our guts, which recent research

is showing has a lot to do with maintaining a healthy weight and keeping your immune system working the way it is supposed to.

- When you eat a plant-based diet and avoid animal foods, you burn calories faster after each meal. Research has shown that people following vegan diets amp up their after-meal metabolism by 16 percent for three or more hours. So that means if you change absolutely nothing else, you're burning more calories by opting for nutrient-dense, fiber-rich vegan food.

YOU LOOK FREAKING AMAZING

One of the first and most obvious benefits of eliminating animal products from your diet will show on your face.

It's no coincidence that dermatologists routinely recommend eliminating dairy to combat acne, particularly in young people. There's increasing evidence of a correlation between our diets and skin breakouts, especially when those diets contain a lot of dairy, fat, and high-glycemic (aka sugary) foods. There's a very famous and well-respected study called the Nurses' Health Study in which the researchers tracked over 47,000 nurses and their health habits, and they found that the ones who drank the most milk when they were teens had much higher rates of acne than those who had little or no milk growing up. The culprits are the hormones and lactose, another name for sugar that is naturally present in

> *Physically, I feel a lot cleaner. My skin cleared up and I stopped getting that kind of grogginess in your stomach after eating. I felt lighter, and I had more energy as well. I honestly never expected this, but it was a pleasant surprise. —Lydia, Hartland, ME*

dairy, which can make your skin flare up and go crazy. And guess what? If you are thinking you can avoid this by opting for skim milk, it was actually fat-free skim milk that had the strongest correlation to acne. That's because skim milk has more naturally occurring sugar and hormones than whole milk, and that hot mess presents a big problem for your skin. (And health. And waistline.)

Beyond all that stuff, if you're anything like me, once you think about drinking breast milk from another species, you'll probably just get grossed out at the thought of it. I mean, would you even want to drink your own mother's milk at this point in your life? Disgusting, right? Well, at least your own mother is not a poor, dirty cow who spends her whole miserable life

> *I absolutely feel better since going vegan. I used to always be someone who was tired and could easily sleep for 12 hours a night. I have so much more energy now, even my family has seen a difference. A lot of my acne has also cleared up and I know for a fact this is due to cutting dairy products.*
> —Laine, Peotone, IL

hooked up to a machine, getting painful infections that contaminate her milk with blood and pus. (Yup, there's a reason milk is sterilized and pasteurized.) A nice glass of soy, coconut, cashew, or almond milk is sounding pretty good about now, right?

For your skin's sake, in addition to avoiding dairy, steer clear of junk food and sodas, stay hydrated (aim for eight to ten glasses of water per day), and eat a nutrient-rich, balanced diet with lots of fruits and vegetables. The high water content in foods like cucumbers, apples, and celery will hydrate your skin, while vitamin C–rich foods like strawberries, oranges, lemons, kale, and cauliflower rev up production of collagen (which keeps skin plump and elastic), leading to smooth and bright skin.

ENVIRONMENT

You understand that climate change is real and getting increasingly dangerous. You care about the environment. Maybe you try to recycle and repurpose instead of waste. As much as you can, you make choices that consider the environment, because you want to make sure that there will always be clean water to drink and fresh air to breathe—not only for you, but for generations to come. If you want to take that love and concern for your planet even further, you might want to consider the huge environmental impact of animal agriculture— the farming of animals for meat, dairy, and eggs.

LOVE YOUR BODY, LOVE YOUR MOTHER EARTH

A few years ago, the United Nations released a groundbreaking report called *Livestock's Long Shadow* that concluded that livestock production causes more greenhouse gasses than all the fossil fuel used for transportation. Seriously. Think about it. Raising food animals causes more environmental depletion than all the trains, planes, trucks, and cars *in the world*. So yes, driving an electric car is a good thing, but saying no to animal foods is way better.

In that report, the UN reported that animal agriculture produces about 18 percent of all global warming gases; but when scientists from the World Bank took a closer look at what goes into raising, transporting, slaughtering, and selling the

> *I realized after going dairy free that my throat was much clearer (less phlegm). I also felt a sense of empowerment as I aligned my consumption patterns with my ethics and shared my passion with family and friends.* —Beau, Portland, OR

animals, they determined that the number was actually more like 51 percent over the full life cycle of the animals. Take a moment here, because this is quite stunning:

> More than half of the problem of climate change can be attributed to our diet of meat, dairy, and eggs.

Robert Goodland and Jeff Ahnang, the World Bank scientists, analyzed each step along the way to our dinner plate, from growing feed (alfalfa, soy, wheat, etc.) for the animals, to the CO_2 emissions that come from tilling the soil, to the methane emissions that come from the animals' waste, to the carbon emissions coming from vehicles transferring animals and refrigerating their flesh. Even their very breaths, burps, and farts produce methane. (I know

> *I lost a few pounds, stopped getting frequent headaches, and cleared my body acne. However, the greatest change was emotionally and spiritually. I felt so good that I was finally living without hurting anyone else. I felt that all my life, my existence had been dependent on harming others, but now, I was finally living free from inflicting intentional harm.* —Lia, Romeoville, IL

it sounds crazy that a cow or chicken can create that much trouble, but the issue is that there are sixty billion animals raised and slaughtered per year in this world. *Sixty billion*. To put that in perspective, there are seven billion humans on the planet. So it's the massive *number* of animals sucking up the resources and polluting the air and water that creates the onerous toll.)

Carbon dioxide tends to be what everyone focuses on in climate change discussions, but methane actually has a global warming potential 86 percent greater than CO2. Animal waste produces nitrous oxide, which is 296 times more destructive than CO2. There's also sulfuric oxide and lots of ammonias and other noxious stuff that comes from their waste. But the biggest problem is that these animals need so much land, either to graze or to produce their feed crops. As a result, the livestock industry bulldozes forests to create pasture and farmland. The problem is that these forests act like holding pens that trap carbon dioxide, so when they're cut down, all that CO2 is released into the atmosphere and climate change ensues, leading to killer floods, storms, fires, and droughts.

Here's the plain and simple truth: The animal food industry is effing up our planet.

Is plant-based agriculture equally problematic? You'll hear a lot of people saying so, but just in the case of water depletion alone, check this out:

Eating 2 slices of cheese is the same as drinking 880 glasses of water.

Producing 1 pound of chicken requires 13 times as much water as producing 1 pound of veggies.

It takes more than 41 times as much water to produce 1 pound of bacon as it does to produce 1 pound of potatoes.

Choosing a ⅓-pound veggie burger over a ⅓-pound beef burger saves almost 600 gallons of water.

Every person who goes vegan can save 600 gallons of water a day.

Thank you to the good people at PETA for those stats!

Animals raised for food produce about ten times more waste than humans do. And you know where all their pee and poop goes? That slop goes into giant lagoons filled to the brim with feces and urine. It's laced with chemicals and antibiotics that then gets sprayed into the air and can contaminate our drinking water and even the plant crops that it's supposed to fertilize.

Each *day*, a person who eats a vegan diet saves roughly forty-five pounds of grain, thirty square feet of forested land, twenty pounds CO2 equivalent, and one animal's life. These stats (and more) are covered in the amazing documentary *Cowspiracy*. I recommend checking out their website to learn more and dive deeper into all the research they've pulled together.

Bottom line: The more meat we eat, the more precious natural resources are used up—really, squandered. I'm sorry, but animal ag's an outdated system. It makes no sense, and over the long run it's simply not sustainable. Something's gotta change, and the sooner, the better.

∼∼∼ SAVE MONEY! ∼∼∼

Consider this: The poorest people in the world, like some of those who lived in the pre–World War II Blue Zones and didn't have a lot of expendable income, primarily ate plant-based diets because they were the most affordable and available foods.

Compared to staple foods like beans, grains, tofu, or most veggies, meat is expensive. Cheese is expensive. Eggs and dairy are expensive, especially if you opt for "organic" or "free range" or "humanely raised." The healthy-but-not-wealthy populations have lived on potatoes and grains and beans and breads and fruits and vegetables for centuries. These are foods you can buy pretty much anywhere, and cheaply. As with all things, if you buy prepared foods, they're going to be more costly, but if you choose simple, whole foods and dress them up with bold, flavorful sauces, you'll actually *save* a ton of dough by eating veganish.

In fact, there is new research just published in the *Journal of Hunger and Environmental Nutrition* that suggests vegetarians can save at least $750 a year when they opt for plant-based meals over meat-based ones. The study calculated those savings by comparing government-recommended weekly meal plans (which include meat) with comparable seven-day plant-based meal plans. And in my experience, the savings are far greater even than that.

We'll take a closer look at how you can eat cheaply on a veganish diet in chapter 3, but for now I'll just say YES YOU CAN!

THE REAL COST OF ANIMAL FOODS

Eating meat, dairy, and eggs is not just expensive in the most obvious sense (what you spend at the grocery store or restaurant), but there are other hidden costs to eating animal products. Did you know that the government actually pays out subsidies to animal producers, which enable them to keep the price of their products artificially low? Yep. Our hard-earned tax money is paying for farmers (I use that term loosely, as these days we're really talking about corporations) to use and abuse animals so they can make more profit. If the government didn't kick in money and deep discounts for animal feed, the livestock industry would be hemorrhaging red ink—or we'd be paying a LOT more for the food we eat.

> *I'm convinced that being a vegetarian has given me emotional strength. It has made me a more confident and happy person. It's something I'm proud of. It's the best decision I ever made. —Zach, Roslyn, NY*

It seems so wrong that an animal's life is reduced to a price tag, especially when that price tag is actually less than the real cost it would take to raise and slaughter it. You have to wonder: *WTF?* Here's the thing: If the government were to stop paying out huge sums of money to animal farmers, the industry would crash and burn. Burgers would be a hundred dollars or more, and you *know* people would not spend that kind of money!

And then there's the cost of what this kind of diet does to our health. Paying to treat people with heart disease and type 2 diabetes is expensive. Drugs and insurance and doctors appointments and surgeries are expensive, and it's time-consuming dealing with them because you miss work or school, or you don't have the energy to live your life the way *you* want to and accomplish all the great things you are capable of.

It's also incredibly expensive to deal with the fallout of climate change (and remember, raising animals is more responsible for climate change than auto emissions and other kinds of transportation pollution). Floods and droughts and all kinds of catastrophic weather events mean people are losing their houses and all of their belongings. Businesses are devastated. Remember Hurricane Sandy in 2012? Scientists say that the monster storm was likely amplified by warmer ocean wa-

> *Commit to it and don't look back. It becomes second nature faster than you would expect. It is a great decision to make for yourself, animals, and the environment. You can absolutely feel the benefits in your everyday life. —Lydia, Hartland, ME*

ters, and that caused over $36 billion in damage to the state of New Jersey. Insurance rates go up to cover those costs or the government has to kick in with money funded by—you guessed it—the taxpayer. It always comes back to us. We pay so much and in so many ways to consume animals.

THE POWER IS YOURS

So, you get my point(s). The old way of eating doesn't work anymore. It's time to move forward, beyond these traditions that have become tired and antiquated. *That* is exciting.

Eating veganish makes sense on a whole lot of levels. It's not just a way of eating, it's a movement. By being part of it, *you* own the path toward positive change. Instead of contributing to suffering, you can live your life in a fully conscious way that benefits the earth, and all the people and animals in it, including yourself!

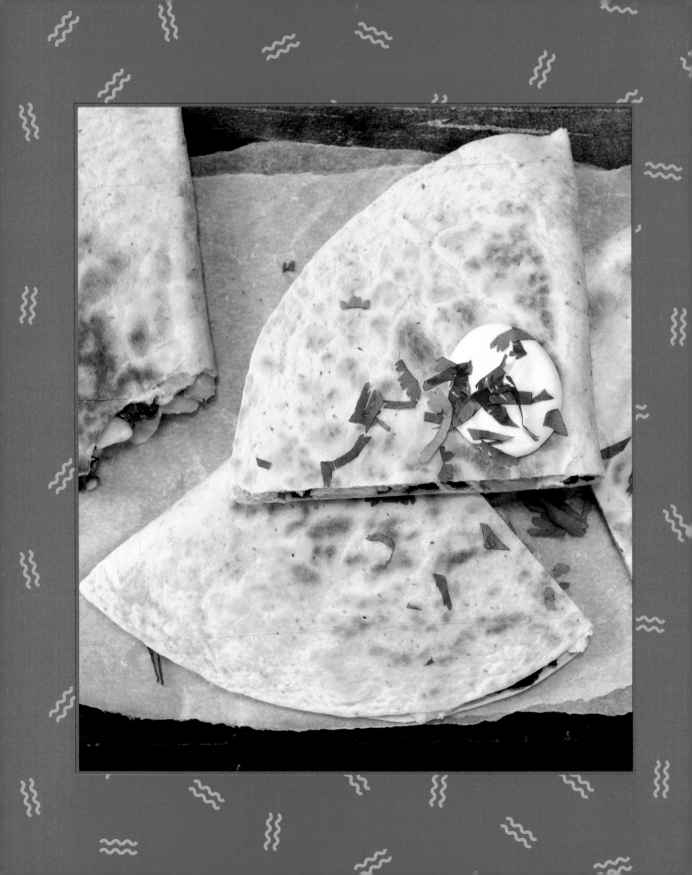

SO I'M VEGANISH.
WHAT THE #!&* DO I EAT?

Now comes the rewarding part.

Let's eat!

Here's the secret: Being veganish is not about what you can't eat. There's nothing you *can't* eat; the difference in moving toward a plant-based diet is simply what you *choose* not to eat. Veganish is about abundance. It's about ADDING IN amazing new foods. It's about how much you get—personally, ethically, environmentally. There's *so much* delicious, healthy food that's not sourced from animals. Discovering what you love and what makes you feel strong and clear-minded is one of the most enjoyable (and tasty!) parts of the veganish adventure.

Take the journey slowly and have fun. You don't have to know where you're ultimately going to end up, or how you'll get there. Set your intention, nudge yourself forward a little, and experiment. Don't overthink it. Just start somewhere and see how it goes. Hello—you're reading this book. You've already started!

Simple swaps are a great first step. Food producers have caught on to how many people choose not to eat animal foods, and you can find a substantial variety of great alternatives to most of the things you're used to eating. Explore your grocery store and see what's out there. Health food and natural foods stores tend to offer the widest variety of plant-based, whole-food staples, but

> *Focus on what in your diet is already vegan rather than what is not. Having simple staples like pasta, rice, beans, and bread at home allows me to mix and match meal ideas on a budget without ever getting bored. Sometimes I resort to a bowl of raisin bran and almond milk in a pinch and remember the first time I tried almond milk and loved it.* —Beau, Portland, OR

increasingly you'll find good options at your regular supermarket, too. As a general rule, you'll find most of what you're looking for in the outer areas of the store—the produce and refrigerated sections—and not in the middle, where mostly boxed and processed foods live.

Wherever you shop, find vegan versions of favorite foods and make them your bridge foods. Replace dairy milk with nondairy milk like almond, cashew, soy, rice, coconut, or hemp. Instead of snacking on dairy cheese, try a vegan cheese like Kite Hill (fancy), Follow Your Heart (mid-priced), or Daiya (very affordable) brands. Use Earth Balance buttery spread on your morning toast, and Vegenaise (it's vegan mayo!) on your sandwiches. These days there are substitutes for just about every meat product: veg-

> *Veganism shouldn't be about "giving up." You're really just finding things you like that replace the things you used to like—just not from an animal. —Ryan, Ventura, CA*

gie bacon strips or sausage patties, tofu hot dogs, chickenless nuggets, juicy meatless quarter-pound burgers! There are so many ways to add the satisfying meaty flavors and textures to food without resorting to actual animal meat.

> *My favorite tip for vegan baking is using 1 tablespoon of ground flax seeds and 3 tablespoons of water to replace one egg. —Dana, East Brunswick, NJ*

Once you've got a few of these simple swap-outs in your fridge, it will be a breeze to veganize one meal per day. For breakfast, have oatmeal with almond milk and fresh fruit, or a tofu scramble with a side of veggie sausage. Have a veggie burger made with lentils or black beans, with a side of sweet potato fries, for lunch or dinner. Swap your spaghetti with meat sauce for spaghetti with veggies and mushrooms (mushrooms are "meaty" and hearty, so I like using them where I used to have meat).

> *Stay strong about your decisions. And make your own choice, on your own time. Know your body. Most people think this "transition" is hard, the food is bad, and they could never give up meat or dairy. Know that it is not hard, and the food is amazing. —Heather, Los Angeles, CA*

SWAP THIS	FOR THAT
Chicken	Tempeh, tofu, meat alternatives in the freezer section
Meat burgers	Veggie burgers
Beef	Beans, veggie "beef" crumbles
Bacon/Sausage	Tempeh or seitan bacon, veggie sausage
Ice cream	Ice cream made with nondairy milks. There are a ton of them that are so good. Sorbet Frozen banana pureed with a touch of almond milk in the food processor or blender!
Milk	Almond, soy, rice, coconut, hemp, hazelnut, cashew, oat, etc.
Butter	Vegan butters (such as Earth Balance), extra-virgin olive oil, avocado Fruit butters, nut butters
Cheese	Nondairy cheese, homemade cashew nut cheese, avocado, hummus (great on sandwiches!)
Eggs	Tofu for scrambles For baking: applesauce, flax, agar (it's seaweed!), chia, banana, vegan egg replacers
Cold cuts	Sliced tofu Veggie meat slices in the refrigerated case Avocado, hummus, PBJ for sandwiches
Half-and-half/Heavy cream	Soy or coconut creamer (mixes with coffee so much better than plain old soy or almond milk)
Cream cheese/Sour cream	Vegan cream cheese/sour cream
Yogurt	Yogurt made from coconut, almond, or soy milk

GREAT START! KEEP GOING!

Once you've committed to one vegan meal per day, try making it two, even three once in a while.

Continue to switch out a few more animal foods for plant-based alternatives each week. If you've already swapped dairy milk for nondairy, next try dairy yogurt and cheese replacements. If you're not ready to totally eliminate meat from your diet, cut out eggs. (On an ethical level, reducing or cutting out eggs is actually an ideal place to begin, even before transitioning away from meat, since egg-laying hens are subjected to some of the worst torture in animal agriculture.)

> Prioritize patience, your values, and forgive yourself if you slip up. It's okay to take time to make the transition as well. It's a beautiful, life-altering decision, and it often takes people a while to make it work.
> —Evan, Mount Vernon, NY

Give yourself fun challenges, like: This week I am going to research on Yelp or Google the best veggie burgers or nondairy ice cream in my area. Today I am going to load up my burrito with everything but meat. Tomorrow I'm going to experiment with a totally new vegetarian soup or salad combination. I am going to become best friends with different kinds of beans and lentils.

> Ease into it. I can't count the number of people I've met who say, "I really want to give up meat, but I don't know if I can, it's just so good!" If you start off with a couple meatless days of the week, you can ease yourself off the habit, eventually (ideally) getting down to meat only a few times a month, and then cutting it out altogether. And even if you don't manage to cut out meat entirely, even cutting down on meat is still a good thing! A lot of people feel intimidated by the idea of adopting vegetarianism or veganism because they feel that it's all or nothing, but the less meat people eat, the better! Even if a person is still eating meat one day out of the week, that's six days of meat that they're not eating. Good for them! —Ben, College Park, MD

DON'T MAKE YOURSELF CRAZY— KEEP IT SIMPLE

When you're first trying a plant-based diet, figuring out how to build a full meal can be confusing. To simplify things, I follow this easy formula for a healthy, hearty meal:

> Protein + Starch + Veggie + Flavor Boost

So easy! The protein and starch keep you full and strong, the veggies give you fiber and nutrients, and the flavor boost takes the taste over the top. Just mix and match your favorite ingredients from the buckets below and you will always end up with something balanced and nutritious that tastes really, really good.

BUCKET 1: PROTEIN

- lentils, chickpeas, black beans, black-eyed peas, etc. (You can buy them in a can, ready to rinse and heat, or cook them from scratch, which is supereasy but takes a bit of planning.)
- tofu
- tempeh (fermented soy cake; found near the tofu in your grocery store)
- edamame (green soy beans in the pod, usually sold frozen)
- meat alternatives (veggie sausage, burgers, or bacon, stocked in the vegetarian section of your grocery store, or vegan chicken and pork, found in the freezer section)
- nuts, nut butter, seeds

BUCKET 2: STARCH

- rice: brown, white, basmati, short grain for sushi, risotto
- quinoa (a seed that looks and tastes like a grain but with more protein)
- pasta (preferably made from whole grains like rice or quinoa pasta, especially if you need to be careful about gluten)
- sweet potatoes
- potatoes
- corn and flour tortillas (Be sure to read the ingredient list, as some very authentic tortillas are made with lard, aka pork fat!)
- any whole grain like millet, barley, wheat berries, bulgur, oats, or whatever you find!

It took me a few months to fully transition to a vegan diet. I started by switching one meal a day to a vegan meal. Then, once that seemed easy, I tried to go the full day only eating vegan foods. Then I would see how many days I could go only eating vegan and it eventually just stuck.
—Sarah, Bloomington, IN

BUCKET 3: VEGGIES

- frozen veggies like broccoli, Brussels sprouts, peas, kale, veggie combination packages (Frozen is just as nutritious as fresh because the veggies are flash-frozen very soon after they are harvested.)
- fresh veggies like cauliflower, green beans, eggplant, asparagus, bell peppers, squash, zucchini, carrots, beets, parsnips; go to a farmers' market or stroll through the supermarket and buy whatever is in season!
- lettuces like arugula, red leaf, and romaine, or any dark, leafy greens like kale or chard

I gave myself about a month to transition. During this time, I figured out what vegan foods I liked and didn't like, what recipes were quick and easy, and what candy I could eat as I have a major sweet tooth.
—Christina, Boca Raton, FL

BUCKET 4: FLAVOR BOOST

- extra-virgin olive oil, pinch of salt, and/or garlic (my fave)
- Sriracha hot sauce
- Thai peanut sauce
- roasted nuts, sesame seeds, sunflower seeds, pumpkin seeds

- vegan Caesar or vegan ranch dressing (Check out the recipes in the back of this book!)
- liquid amino acids (such as Bragg brand), a liquid similar to soy sauce (and similarly made from soybeans and purified water) that gives a tasty added protein and amino acid nutrient boost to food
- soy sauce or tamari (gluten-free soy sauce)
- avocado, hummus
- vegan pesto
- nutritional yeast (Shake on some of these flakes for a Parmesan-like cheesy flavor.)

> *I am crazy for garlic quinoa. After I make the quinoa, I melt some Earth Balance vegan butter and mix in a bunch of garlic powder. Then I put the garlic butter into my bowl of quinoa and add some veggies like eggplant or peppers. Great for a quick meal if you're in a hurry. —Lydia, New York, NY*

While you are getting familiar and comfortable with cooking and eating in a new way, this formula will keep it super simple and easy to organize when you're grocery shopping or thinking of what you want to eat. Just keep some favorite sauces in your fridge, and you can make just about anything taste good, pronto. You can order with this equation in mind at restaurants, too. Bean burrito with guac and salsa, hold the cheese. Thai veggies and tofu over rice with a squeeze of Sriracha. Veggie sushi with edamame and a squeeze of liquid aminos or soy sauce. Baked potato and baked beans with all kinds of veggies on top and a dollop of Thai peanut sauce, with a side of garlicky beans. See the formula in there? Plant-based protein + starch + veggie + flavor boost = a happy meal.

Although you're going to discover some amazing recipes in this book, you may not always (or ever) be up for following a recipe step-by-step, and that's just fine. Simple, no-recipe meals will keep your food spending really low, won't tax your time, and will provide you with healthy, hearty, and tasty meals. Going veganish is easy when you're chill about it!

> *One of my favorite quick meals is a "Buddha bowl." Grains, like quinoa or brown rice, roasted veggies, hummus, maybe some avocado, a protein like tofu or beans, and some sort of sauce to tie it all together. They are so delicious and nutrient-dense! —Emily, Weston, MA*

I keep potatoes on hand to microwave if I'm in a hurry; they're really satisfying with something simple like baked beans on top. Then I'll do a salad on the side. I swing by the grocery store once a week and stock my fridge and freezer with veggies and meat replacements, so I'm never gazing into an empty fridge or pantry; that just makes it too tempting to pick up the phone and order a pizza!

WHAT DOES AN EASY VEGAN MEAL LOOK LIKE?

Mix-and-Match Meal Suggestions

BREAKFAST		
BASE	**PLUS**	**MAYBE ALSO PLUS**
Cereal	Almond milk	Dried fruits (raisins, goji berries)
Granola	Rice milk	Fresh fruits (banana, berries)
Rolled oats	Soy milk	Frozen fruits (berries), nuts
Brown rice	Coconut milk	Chopped dates, nuts
Quinoa	Hemp milk	Dried fruits, chopped nuts
		Seeds (hemp, pumpkin, chia)
Scrambled tofu	Mushrooms	Spread out on toast, or with potatoes
	Spinach	Veggie bacon or sausage
	Tomatoes	
	Zucchini	
	Sweet potatoes	

LUNCH/DINNER		
Burger/Sandwich	Tomato	Cashew nut cheese
	Leafy greens (kale, spinach, lettuce)	Daiya vegan cheese
	Sprouts	Hummus
	Avocado	Sliced and grilled tofu
	Pickle	Grilled mushrooms
		Grilled onions
		Vegenaise mayo, mustard
Bowl of beans (black, red, pinto) or lentils	Soy sauce	Sautéed or steamed veggies (You can use frozen!)
Brown rice	Hot sauce	Baked sweet potato
Quinoa	Extra-virgin olive oil and garlic	Tons of salad
Couscous	Dairy-free pesto sauce	
	Tahini sauce	
	Tofu	
	Tempeh	
	Seitan	

By the way, I'm obsessed with Instagramming my food, so please feel free to check out my page (and the people I follow)—www.instagram.com /kathyfreston—for more vegan-eating tips and inspiration! And tag your pics #eatingveganish so I can see what you're cooking up, too!

You'll find even more charts with breakfast and sandwich combinations in chapter 7 of this book!

> *I love nutritional yeast. It is a "seasoning" that consists of yellowish flakes and can make anything "cheesy." I add it to rice with some vegan butter or olive oil and you have cheesy rice (very cheap). I make vegan mac and cheese with it.*
> *—Rachel, Philadelphia, PA*

∼∼∼ NO FOOD PROCESSOR? ∼∼∼ NO PROBLEM!

Don't think you need to have a tricked-out kitchen to make veganish meals. I throw simple foods together according to my mood, and I don't need fancy equipment to do so. My kitchen is pretty lean and mean, and I can easily make all the food I need to have three great vegan meals a day with a little bit of planning. For example, I use a rice cooker to make rice or whatever grain I fancy a couple times each week so that I always have some on hand in the fridge to use throughout the week as a base for my meals. I also eat it for breakfast warmed and topped with chopped dates, sliced bananas, and nuts.

> *If you can't think of anything to eat for lunch or dinner, you could always make some veggie stir-fry. Just chop up some vegetables that you like, add some rice and beans, and cook them all together, on the stovetop in a frying pan. And if you just want a snack, I recommend some soy, almond, or coconut yogurt with granola and fruit. —Caroline, Cincinnati, OH*

Besides my trusty rice cooker (and honestly, a plain old saucepan can do the job as well; you just have to pay a little more attention!), I use a skillet for veggies or grilled tofu, a toaster oven for potatoes or a cheesy toast snack, and sometimes I put my slow cooker to use. This very cool, inexpensive appliance lets you throw some ingredients together in the morning and leave the food to slowly simmer; by lunch or dinner you have a superdelicious hot meal. A few pots and pans for steaming veggies, cooking pasta, or making soup, and that's about it.

CASHEW CREAM

I'm going to impart a little nugget of culinary genius that I learned from my friend Chef Tal Ronnen. Cashew milk and cashew cream are insanely easy to make on your own. You don't even need a recipe for them: Just take a handful of raw, unsalted cashews and cover them with water and soak them overnight. In the morning, drain off the water and put them in a high-speed blender with some fresh water and BLEND. The amount of water needed depends on how thick you want the cashew cream to be. The more powerful the blender, the better, so that the result is super-duper creamy. You can use this for creamy pasta sauces or as a soup base; or you can sweeten it with a little agave or maple syrup and add fruit for a fab gourmet-like dessert served in a martini glass!

SERIOUSLY, EAT YOUR VEGGIES

So you've swapped out some dairy products and maybe even stopped eating eggs, chicken, or beef. The next superimportant step in transitioning to your veganish diet is committing to adding as many vegetables as possible to your meals. The more veggies you eat, the more you'll get to like them, promise!

If you'd told my younger self that I would actually seek out anything green and leafy, I'd have called you crazy. I went to great lengths to avoid eating vegetables. We didn't have a lot of money when I grew up, so our kitchen table was fashioned out of a giant cable spool that my dad had found at a nearby construction site. It had little

Cashew mac 'n' cheese: Blend cashews, water, garlic, and nutritional yeast and pour over noodles for a delicious and supereasy mac 'n' cheese.
—Tess, Walnut Creek, CA

holes on and around the three-foot-wide stem and was hollow on the inside, making it the perfect place for me to stuff broccoli and spinach into when my parents weren't looking. (When we moved years later, there were disgusting wads of mummified veggies in there.) So I get it; not everyone is born loving vegetables. Back then, my mom only had cans of greens that she'd boil and put on our plates, telling us to eat them because they were good for us. *Not* a great sales pitch, then or now.

> *One of my quickest and favorite meals consists of roasting vegetables and mixing them in with pasta, vegan green pesto, tomato puree, and nutritional yeast. It involves minimal preparation and cooking time and is really tasty.*
> —Eve, Glasgow, Scotland

But your tastes can change. Mine did. I adore vegetables now, and love the variety of colors and textures they add to my meals, along with making each meal more nutrient-dense and filling. I actually crave them so much that I've found a number of ways to sneak more veggies into my diet—by choice! If you're not coming into this as a vegetable lover, here are a few tricks for finding what works for you.

- Buy big bags of frozen kale, spinach, and broccoli, and add a heaping handful to your daily smoothie. That right there counts for two servings of veggies, even when what you're mostly tasting is the peanut butter or blueberries or whatever else is in the shake. (When the veggies are frozen, you can't taste them in a smoothie.)

> *The same way you wouldn't eat steak all day every day, you shouldn't do that with vegan pizza. Meaning, don't set yourself up to fail and become unhealthy. If done right, a plant-based diet can be your health's most powerful ally.* —Katherine, Tempe, AZ

- Condiments are a good way to flavor up a simple meal of grains and veggies. My fridge always has soy sauce, Sriracha, Thai peanut sauce, and vegan ranch dressing, so I can just microwave or sauté whatever greens are on hand, and add a squirt or shake of something to make the veggies even more delicious.
- Garlic and extra-virgin olive oil with a pinch of salt can make just about anything taste fantastic, especially sautéed greens.
- Some people are genetically programmed to find the taste of broccoli really bitter, but if you squeeze a little lemon juice onto it, it nullifies the bitterness. Cool, right?

- Put spinach, kale, or other leafy greens into your burger patties or sandwich buns.
- Throw in some finely chopped veggies if you're making any kind of soup or stew.
- Chop cauliflower really fine so that it looks like rice. I sauté it with some sun-dried tomatoes, olives, and onions, and then add some grilled tofu or a meat replacement on top, and it totally feels like I'm eating a mound of rice, which makes this simple, delicious meal seem decadent and not just nutritious!

Veggies are your number one source for the vitamins and minerals your body needs to do its work and keep you looking and feeling your best; they're like scrub brushes cleaning out your body and nourishing it with nutrients. They're loaded with antioxidants, which stave off all kinds of diseases and maladies and keep your skin glowing and gorgeous. And as much as vitamin companies would have you believe you can get everything from a pill, supplements are nowhere near as beneficial as vitamins delivered naturally to your body in the form of whole foods.

Once you and veggies are ready to progress from the flirtation stage to a full-on relationship, hit the farmers' market. Some stands offer samples, so try everything green or colorful! Pick up an item that you've never eaten before from the produce section of your supermarket and take it home to experiment with. Try a veggie menu item from a restaurant or a recipe that sounds intriguing. Don't like cauliflower or kale? That's okay. Just focus on veggies that speak to your own palate and that get you excited about eating all that goodness. Don't worry about what's trendy on restaurant menus. You'll never get bored eating nutritious whole foods if you challenge yourself to find exciting foods that just taste good to you. And I guarantee you're going to find stuff you'll love!

I was a very bad vegetarian for a while. Though I did my research, I did not always eat very balanced. I would grab grilled cheeses and cheese pizza and other things that were not healthy. I ended up gaining weight. But once I went vegan, I lost 10 pounds. Not because I was eating less, but because I was just not eating all the fat that came along with dairy cheese. I guess what I am trying to say is that my mistake was thinking that I was automatically eating okay since the food had no meat on it. We still have to be careful as vegetarians and vegans and make sure that we are eating the right amount of vegetables, calcium, protein, and all that good stuff. —Suzeii, Weslaco, TX

AND TAKE THAT VITAMIN B12. SERIOUSLY.

If you decide to go completely vegan, you're going to feel great. You'll have more energy. You'll lose some weight if you're carrying extra. If you have acne, there's a good chance it'll clear up. But after you've been vegan for a while, you'll want to make sure you're getting some supplemental B12. It's a micronutrient that helps keep your nerves and blood cells healthy. We need very little B12, but we do need it; and it's the only nutrient that you can't get in a vegan diet.

B12 is actually not made by animals or plants. It is made by bacteria. Some people speculate that years ago, the traces of bacteria in soil or on vegetables would produce the B12 we need. But that is certainly not the case today, if it ever was. Animals have bacteria in their intestinal tracts that produce B12. And some of that B12 passes into meat or milk. But many people don't absorb that very well. The B12 in supplements (such as typical multivitamins) is very absorbable. Cool fact, though: All B12 supplements are vegan, because manufacturers make it straight from micro-organisms—no animal necessary. So take that B12 (or eat B12-fortified foods). It's cheap and easy to find!

HEALTHY EATING 101

- Opt for GOOD carbs. Carbohydrates are the sugars, starches, and fiber found in foods. They have a bad rep these days, but not all carbs are created equal. It's refined carbs, those in highly processed foods, that we want to avoid. Unrefined carbs are good when you eat them in reasonable quantities. Unrefined and unprocessed means the food hasn't been pulverized, broken down, pumped with chemicals and additives; it's just the whole food as nature created it. Let's take oats as an example. Whole steel-cut oats haven't been pulverized into flour and then reconstituted with other ingredients to become a cereal like Cheerios. Unrefined oats are still intact, with all of their natural fiber so the carbohydrates are absorbed slowly into our systems. There's no spike in blood sugar levels as there is when you eat a highly refined carb, which goes right into your bloodstream. You might get a burst of energy from that, but as fast as your blood sugar spikes, it drops just as quickly, leaving you cranky and hungry—and looking for more "quick fix" energy from stuff like cereal, pastries, and sweets. It's fattening and maddening and not a fun roller coaster to be riding. Good carbs come from whole potatoes and other root vegetables like yams, beets, and parsnips; brown rice and any whole grains; quinoa; beans; vegetables; and fruit.

- Steer clear of BAD carbs, which are refined, meaning they no longer resemble the food they came from. When food is refined, it's altered to increase the shelf life of the product, usually by eliminating certain things like good fats (which can go rancid over time). Refined food is usually higher in calories, and you're getting stuff you don't want like high-fructose corn syrup and all kinds of weird fillers. When food is unrefined, it breaks down in your body slowly, so the glucose (aka sugar) is dispersed little by little and you get steady fuel to keep your energy up. Think of it this way: The more refined, or "whiter," the grain-based food, the lower the fiber. (Whole-grain pastas and corn tortillas are fine because the processing is minimal.)

- Color your plate. In fruits and veggies, colors are like banners for the nutrients they contain. Consuming a rainbow of fruits and veggies is a great way to be sure you're getting the diversity of vitamins, minerals, and antioxidants you need. Rule of thumb: The more colorful, the better! (Isn't nature brilliant?)

- Hydrate. Every organ in your body requires water, so you'll function optimally if you're well hydrated. Although there's no hard and fast rule on how much you need, generally eight to ten glasses a day will do the trick. Unless you're working out hard and sweating a lot—in that case, keep chugging. Bonus: When you have a glass of H_2O before meals, you'll feel fuller and pig out less. And your skin will be clear and glowing. Don't like plain water? Make herbal iced tea and drink that. Or add a squeeze of lemon or a small splash of your favorite (unsweetened)

> Some of the cookbook recipes I love are the vegetarian chili and pea soup from Laurel's Kitchen; vegan lasagna from Forks Over Knives; yellow dal from Smitten Kitchen. Even easier: Buy MorningStar [Farms] Grillers or Amy's burritos. Two minutes in the microwave. Amazing. —Ben, College Park, MD

fruit juice to your glass of water. Or cut up some cucumbers and put them into a pitcher of water. Soda is loaded with sugar and high-fructose corn syrup (or chemicals if it's "diet" soda), so just avoid them.

- Eat fiber-rich foods. Anything from the plant kingdom has tons of fiber. (Fun fact: Fiber is to plants as bones are to animals.) One more time: Fiber fills your stomach so you're not hungry, it signals your brain that you're satisfied, it helps the food digest more slowly and evenly, and it helps your blood glucose levels stay even throughout the day so you stay energetic and alert. Fiber also feeds the good bacteria in your gut, which keeps your digestion smooth.

> *Plantains are fantastic for you and very filling. Often times, when I'm in a snag, I will bake a plantain (because frying every day isn't the best), have black beans with fresh tomato and avocado on the side, some mango salsa, and tortillas. It's a fantastic, filling meal that will make you happy you ate it. —Emily, Philadelphia, PA*

- Keep your engine revved. Your metabolism needs to be stoked, starting with a healthy breakfast. Keep it humming with small snacks like nuts and seeds between meals. That way you won't get too hungry and your body won't think you're starving and hold on to every little calorie like it's the last it'll ever get.

- Portion your food. Be sure you see a lot of green on your plate (you can have as much as you want). Make up your plate in the kitchen rather than serving everything family style, which encourages you to take seconds and thirds before you realize your body is full. If a restaurant gives you a giant serving, ask for a to-go container and take half home for lunch the next day. (Or, to be extra environmentally friendly, travel with a reusable takeout container in your backpack or purse.) At home, use salad-size plates so you don't go wild filling up a giant bowl or plate.

- Avoid foods with sugar and/or high-fructose corn syrup. Check labels carefully, because the food companies know that sweet taste is addictive. You are not their puppet—if sugar or high-fructose corn syrup is listed as one of the first five ingredients, just put the package down and back away.

- Don't go crazy with oil. Oil is pure fat, and it damages the endothelial cells that line the insides of your arteries. A little extra-virgin olive oil is okay, but if your plate of food looks slimy or shiny, you're probably using too much oil.

- Take a B12 supplement daily.
- Move your body. Walk really fast, play sports, skate, run with your dog. Get your heart rate up to where your breathing is labored—enough so that it's difficult but not impossible to carry on a conversation. Try to do something active six days a week (I believe chilling out and resting once a week is mandatory!) so that your energy is regularly revved. I love to hike and ride my bike, but sometimes I just close my bedroom door, blast some music, and dance my ass off. (Weddings are good for that, too!) Whatever gets your blood pumping is great—just do it!

NUTRITION BASICS: YOU GET THIS FROM THAT

We're told all the time to eat nutritious foods, but what does that really mean? Here's a breakdown of the essential vitamins and minerals your body needs to do its best work. Next time you hear the phrase "color your plate" for nutritional value, think of how vibrantly colorful these foods are!

VITAMIN/MINERAL	BENEFITS	FOUND IN
Vitamin A	Bone growth, eye health, immune system and preventing infections	Carrots, dark green leafy vegetables, bell peppers, dried apricots
Beta carotene	An antioxidant that converts in the body to vitamin A	Carrots, sweet potatoes, yams, pumpkins, spinach, collard greens, turnip greens, mangoes
Vitamin B1 (thiamin)	Converts food into energy; promotes healthy skin, hair, brain, and muscles	Acorn squash, soy milk, watermelons, sunflower seeds, navy beans, black beans, pinto beans, lentils, barley, dried peas, oats

VITAMIN/MINERAL	BENEFITS	FOUND IN
Vitamin B2 (riboflavin)	Converts food into energy; promotes healthy skin, hair, brain, and blood	Whole and fortified grains and cereals, peanut butter, potatoes, mushrooms, soybeans, spinach, beet greens, asparagus, almonds
Vitamin B3 (niacin)	Converts food into energy; promotes healthy skin, hair, brain, blood, and nervous system	Whole and fortified grains and cereals, peanuts, mushrooms, green peas, sunflower seeds, avocados
Vitamin B6	Converts tryptophan to niacin and serotonin, which aids in sleep, appetite, and moods; helps immune function, cognitive abilities, and the making of red blood cells	Bananas, legumes, tofu and other soy products, potatoes, sweet potatoes, spinach, sunflower seeds, and watermelons
Vitamin B12	Essential for cell division and blood formation; aids energy levels	Found in fortified foods such as certain soy milks and breakfast cereals (Read labels carefully, and take a B12 supplement!)
Vitamin C	Aids the growth and repair of tissues in all parts of the body and immune system	Oranges and other citrus, broccoli, cauliflower, spinach, cabbage, potatoes, papaya, bell peppers, Brussels sprouts, strawberries, pineapple, kiwi, cantaloupe
Vitamin D	Regulates the formation of bone and the absorption of calcium and phosphorus from the intestines	Sunlight! Get some, it's free!
Vitamin E	Protects against cell damage; plays a role in immune function and DNA repair	Vegetable oils, wheat germ, avocados, hazelnuts, almonds, sunflower seeds, spinach, Swiss chard, peanuts, asparagus, beet greens

(continued)

VITAMIN/MINERAL	BENEFITS	FOUND IN
Calcium	Needed for strong, healthy bones and teeth and for the working of muscles	Some soy milks, nuts, seeds, green leafy vegetables, tofu, dried fruit, fortified orange juice and cereals (Read labels carefully.)
Iodine	Needed to make thyroid hormones, which control metabolism and many other important body functions	Green leafy vegetables, seaweed, kelp, potatoes, dried prunes, navy beans, bananas, cranberries, green beans
Iron	Needed for healthy red blood cells to transport oxygen	Beans, lentils, dried fruit, whole grains (including bread), molasses, squash, spinach, cabbage, nuts, pumpkin seeds, dark leafy greens, dark chocolate and cocoa powder (hello!), tofu
Magnesium	Promotes healthy muscle function	Whole grains, green leafy vegetables, beans, nuts
Potassium	Aids nerve function, muscle control, and blood pressure	Dried fruit, bananas, potatoes, nuts, beans, peas, lentils, whole grains, wheat germ, almonds, apricots, broccoli, Brussels sprouts, carrots, cantaloupes, dates, nectarines, oranges, raisins, soy milk, strawberries, tomatoes
Selenium	Essential for overall good health and supporting the immune system	Whole grains, beans, peas, lentils, nuts, sunflower seeds
Zinc	Supports normal growth and a healthy immune system; helps heal wounds and maintain sense of taste and smell	Lentils, sesame seeds, pumpkin seeds, brown rice and other whole grains, green vegetables

≈≈ PROTEIN: NOT A PROBLEM ≈≈

Let's really take a minute and talk about protein. As you move toward a plant-based diet, the main concern you will hear from family and friends who aren't vegan or vegetarian is, "But how will you get enough protein?"

I hear that all the time and I get it, because protein is such a major buzzword these days—we seem to have an obsession with it in our culture. You'll hear it from the high-protein, low-carb gang, and even dietitians and doctors who mean well. Granted, those folks are right in that we shouldn't

> *Sriracha tofu is delicious! Just mix some vinegar, soy sauce, and Sriracha together and marinate some tofu in it for a day. Then bake it or fry it. —Radhika, Mukilteo, WA*

be eating all the refined junky carbs and sweet stuff we've been peddled for years, and high-protein, low-carb advocates are certainly right to steer us away from dairy, but they go too far when they tell us to focus so hard on protein, protein, protein. Obviously we need protein, but we shouldn't be *obsessed* with it. Protein is simply a macronutrient found in just about all foods to varying degrees. Health enthusiasts have gotten into a dangerous habit of breaking down food into its component parts rather than looking at things as a whole. By doing that, we miss the complete picture.

Despite what the meat and dairy industries want us to believe, animal products are not the sole or even the best source of protein. The important thing, says the Harvard School of Public Health, is to consider the "protein package"—as in, what else comes along with the

> *One of my favorite foods is tacos, and they are delicious and easy to make. Heat up a base of soy protein crumbles or lard-free refried beans. Add nutritional yeast and some red pepper flakes. If I have it on hand, I add some vegan cheese to the mix. When everything is done, I roll them together in a warm tortilla and enjoy with taco sauce. Sometimes I'll use some salsa as well. —Evan, Mount Vernon, NY*

protein. In the case of meat, dairy, and eggs, you get saturated fat, cholesterol, and zero fiber—and that kind of diet is strongly associated with obesity, type 2 diabetes, heart disease, and certain types of cancer. Those are the primary killers of our time! It's not just Harvard saying that (and certainly not just me!). This finding is supported by nearly every large-scale scientific study of eating habits from around the world. When researchers compare people with meat-rich diets to people who eat very little meat, it's always the same: Big meat eaters tend to be heavier and sicker and don't live as long as the plant-based eaters. Watch the documentary *Forks Over Knives* or read *Proteinaholic* by Dr. Garth Davis to better understand the protein spell we seem to be under. Probably the best and most widely published gold-standard, peer-reviewed studies that looked at hundreds of thousands of people are the Adventist Health Studies, which you can easily find online if you want to see the science right in front of you.

Now to the positive side of the equation: You can get all the protein you need by eating plant-based foods, plus you get tons of fiber, healthy nutrients and antioxidants, zero cholesterol, and not much fat at all. But, okay, let's be really specific and answer that question of *where you're going to get your protein*, because I promise that you will be asked this all the time. Let me acknowledge first that you actually can end up short on protein if you're not paying attention—not enough to deem you medically deficient, but enough to leave you feeling dissatisfied or hungry between meals. If you don't give any consideration to protein at all, and just eat pasta or salads, you're going to feel hungry and maybe even weak. You need beans. You need nuts. You need enough calories from whatever whole foods you're eating to hit your mark.

So how much protein do you actually need?

> The recommended daily protein intake per day is about 56 grams for an adult man, and about 46 grams for an adult woman.

You will get those protein grams from beans like fava, black, kidney, and white beans; and black-eyed peas, chickpeas, and lentils. You get it from seeds like sunflower, flax, hemp, chia, pumpkin, sesame, and quinoa (which people think is a grain but is actually a seed). You supercharge your intake of protein by eating whole nuts like peanuts, cashews, and almonds; and delicious nut butters like peanut butter, almond butter, cashew butter, and tahini (a sesame seed paste used along with chickpeas to make hummus). Protein is also abundant in soy products like tofu and tempeh or in meat substitutes like seitan (wheat protein) or veggie sausage or "chick'n." You'll also get it from all kinds of veggies like kale and broccoli. It's in your pasta and rice, and in just about everything you eat that isn't superprocessed.

> *One of my favorite meals can be as simple as you want it to be, but really delicious and healthy. A mixture of beans, rice, and veggies is one of my go-to dinners. It is high in protein and very filling. I generally buy already cooked kidney, garbanzo, or any other type of beans that come in a can and heat them up, although you can also take the time to cook beans from scratch. I make a pot of brown rice or rice pilaf, and grill or sauté some veggies (carrots, asparagus, zucchini). Sometimes I add extra-virgin olive oil as a sauce once all the items are mixed together in a bowl. I eat this dinner a lot when I am short on time or energy, and it is easy to make extra and save for leftovers because it reheats well. —Madeline, Minneapolis, MN*

And while we're on the subject of protein, let's also talk meat alternatives for a minute, because I often hear, "Oh, but they aren't natural and I don't want to eat fake foods!" Cool, you don't have to. But meat substitutes are a fantastic way to transition away from animal foods and get that protein everyone is always so worried about. Some health sticklers are down on fake meats, but sometimes they scratch an itch that beans or kale just can't. Every once in a while, I feel like I need that traditional meal of turkey and mashed potatoes. Rather than fight it, I'll have "turkey" made from whole grains and plant-based proteins, served with a big old pile of mashed potatoes, and I get my fix. If I'm at a barbecue with friends, I don't want to be eating a bowl of rice and beans while everyone else is filling up their buns. I want a hot dog! I want a burger! So I'm glad there are delicious veg-based burgers and sausages I can slap on the grill and load up with pickles, ketchup, and onions like everyone else. I just don't make them the core of my diet or my main source of protein.

If I'm working out hard and I don't have the time or energy to shop and prepare a real meal with plenty of protein to support my active day, I make a protein smoothie. Since I tend to work and work out hard, I make a smoothie almost every day. It's a shortcut, but it works. Find your favorite vegan protein powder and blend it up with some coconut water or soy milk, throw in some peanut or almond butter and some fresh or frozen fruit and *voilà*, you'll feel satisfied!

> *I have no difficulty getting enough protein in my diet. Quick supplements like rice protein powder, which is vegan, make it easy to add protein to smoothies. —Laura, Seattle, WA*

Oh, and I *always* throw in a handful of frozen greens for some extra nutrition. (See the smoothie recipe builder on page 69.)

So, long story short, there's a bunch of different ways to get healthy protein, and I get it by eating a rich variety of lots of different healthy foods!

THE CASE FOR GLUTEN

I'm sure you've heard all the hoopla about gluten and are wondering if you should be going gluten-free too. Gluten is a term that describes the proteins found in wheat, rye, barley, and foods made with these grains. For some people, it can cause problems like bloating, stomach pain, fatigue, diarrhea, as well as pain in the bones and joints. For people with an autoimmune disorder called celiac disease, the ingestion of gluten leads to damage in the small intestine. Fortunately, celiac is quite rare—only about 1 percent of the population has it. But since gluten is found in a lot of bready processed foods like pizza, cookies, and burger buns that won't do your body proud *anyway*, it's not a bad idea to limit foods containing gluten. You can get tested to see if you're intolerant of gluten, but the tests are not always conclusive. Best to avoid all wheat and wheat products for six to eight weeks, see how you feel, and then make your own decision. If you do decide to avoid gluten, check the labels of meat alternatives, because they often have gluten in them. Seitan, for example, is pure wheat gluten (but super high in protein!). Beyond Meat and Sunshine Burgers are gluten-free, though; and Gardein has a bunch of gluten-free items, too.

I don't have a problem processing gluten, but I try to avoid it anyway because the foods it's in can be fattening. But full disclosure: One of my favorite snacks is toasted German black bread (it's that really dark, thin bread made mostly from rye and barley) with either peanut butter or sliced avocado and tomato on top. That makes my belly very happy! So while I try to limit my intake, I don't make myself crazy about eating totally gluten-free, either.

WHOLE FOODS ARE WHOLLY AWESOME

Remember Lloyd Dobler's classic rant from the movie *Say Anything*? "I don't want to sell anything bought or processed, or buy anything sold or processed, or process anything sold, bought, or processed . . ."

Go, Lloyd.

When it comes to food, just keep it simple. Choose things that have grown in the ground or on trees. Choose foods that wouldn't break your heart bringing them to table. For instance, it's quite pleasant to dig potatoes from the ground, or pick berries from a bush, or cut and chop kale or broccoli. It's quite disgusting and disturbing to push a squealing animal toward the slaughter line and pro-

> As much as I can, I try to eat whole foods. I like to eat apples, carrots, nuts, bananas, melon, and spiced quinoa for snacks. I love stir-fry vegetables with a bit of soy sauce. I also like to make quinoa and pinto beans as a quick meal.
> —Tyler, Columbus, OH

cess its flesh through scalding tanks, eviscerating machines, and chopping blocks. One process is peaceful and rewarding; the other is painful. I'll take peacefully produced foods any time, thank you very much. My rule of thumb is that I'll eat something if it doesn't make me sick to think about how it got to my plate. Simple, right?

It irks me when people say, "Oh, I only want to eat food my grandmother would recognize." Well, my grandmother would certainly recognize ham, but eating it isn't cool with me because I'm not comfortable with the *process* that pig went through to get to my plate. My grandmother also lived during a time when racial segregation and sexual preference discrimination were accepted, so let's not pretend that the "old" way is always the best way.

Yes, it's true we should avoid foods with a long list of ingredients on the package, because for the most part, the longer the list, the further that food is from its natural state. Too much sugar, salt, chemicals, and fat is certainly not good, and making a habit of processed foods flips your taste buds out so they can't even appreciate the simple (healthy) stuff anymore. Sugar, fat, and salt trigger a dopamine (the neurotransmitter that signals something good is happening) response in the brain, so you just end up wanting to eat more, more, more of the same kind of processed, sweet, fatty stuff. Which makes you fat, tired, and addicted.

The fewer ingredients a packaged food has, the better it will be for your health (and waistline). The bottom line is that you're better off eating as many whole, plant-based foods as possible, because they're packed with naturally occurring vitamins and our superhero, *fiber*. Bottom line: While some hard-core health fanatics might take issue with processed meat alternatives, frankly, I'd much rather see you eat veggie sausage than "real" sausage made from an animal.

CAN I AFFORD TO BE VEGAN?

You *absolutely* can!

Eating vegan is cheap when you keep it simple. The staples of a plant-based diet—rice, beans, potatoes, and veggies—are among the least expensive foods, *period*. My friend Darshana Thacker over at *Forks Over Knives* decided she wanted to see what it was like to live on $1.50 a day so that she could better relate to people who struggle with getting enough to eat for the money they make. She also wanted to see if it was possible to eat healthfully (in her mind that means plant-based!) on such an austere budget. Darshana took into account the accessibility of food items, the time it took to make a meal, and what she could actually buy with her allotted budget. Darshana had $7.50 to spend for five days, and she made most of her purchases at her local 99¢ store. There, she bought:

- 10-pound bag of potatoes = 99¢
- 2-pound bag of carrots = 99¢
- 1-pound bag of brown rice = 99¢
- 1-pound bag of brown lentils = 99¢
- ⅔ pound of brown rice pasta = 99¢
- 2 cans of tomato sauce = 99¢

She also bought ½ pound of organic oatmeal from the bulk section of a health food store for 42¢. She then set aside 30¢ for some spices from her pantry.

In her words, this is what she ate for five days:

- Day 1: Masala mashed potatoes and lentil stew with spices, carrots, and brown rice. I divided it into three meals, which was plenty for the day. I even had leftovers!
- Day 2: Oatmeal with carrots, boiled potatoes seasoned with salt and pepper, leftover lentil stew and fresh carrots. Again, I had plenty to eat.
- Day 3: Potato stew with tomato sauce, leftover brown rice and lentil stew, and fresh carrots.
- Day 4: Baked potatoes, brown rice with carrots, curry-flavored oatmeal with carrots, sprouted lentil dal. I really enjoyed my food this day—sprouting the lentils made them taste fresh and light, and baked potatoes are so good! I bought a lime this day for 33¢ (pricey for one lime!), because I was missing sour flavors.
- Day 5: Pasta with tomato sauce, lentils, and carrots, plus baked potatoes. And I spent the remaining 45¢ on ½ pound of fresh organic spinach! There was enough pasta left over for lunch the next day. I also ended up with about two pounds of unused potatoes.

Get a support system going. Reach out to that vegetarian or vegan you already know and get their advice and tips so that they can help you out on the way.
—Ryan, Ventura, CA

I love making a big pot of veggie chili—just throw in a bunch of vegetables, beans, tomatoes, spices, and let it all simmer. Then I keep this in the fridge with some steamed rice. I tend to be pretty busy during the week, and this way I can just throw some rice and chili in the microwave, top it with avocado, and I have a fast and healthy dinner. —Laine, Peotone, IL

She said that the experiment of eating on a low budget oriented her toward simple, unprocessed food. She felt totally full and satisfied, and was actually really energized by the whole experience. She walked away from it with an awareness that "in order to feed a hungry world we need to focus our resources on simple starchy staple foods, which provide the highest number of reasonably nutritious calories for the least amount of money."

Clearly, you don't need to be as extreme as Darshana's experiment, but she did it to prove that you can indeed be nourished and satisfied for very little money. This is really good news for students and anyone on a budget!

AFFORDABLE VEGAN CHECKLIST

Here are some suggestions for making it work without blowing your budget:

- Make a list of the most affordable foods (like sweet potatoes and brown rice) that appeal to your taste buds, and use them as the foundation for your meals.
- When you shop, go armed with a list of items by category (such as proteins, fruits, vegetables, starches, snacks, etc.) so you can shop more effectively and not get sidetracked by impulse purchases.
- Speaking of impulse spending, try to shop on a full stomach so you're less likely to overspend on foods your stomach wants in that moment but your wallet can't necessarily afford.
- Frozen fruits and vegetables are fantastic, cheap alternatives to fresh. They're flash-frozen right at harvest, so they often retain more nutrients than the fresh produce shipped from halfway around the world.
- Ask the folks at your farmers' market for their "seconds" (the slightly bruised but still very tasty fruits and vegetables that other customers won't necessarily buy). They usually cost much less than the "pretty" produce, but taste just as good. Just make sure to use them up right away, as bruised fruit especially can rot quickly.
- Volunteer at a garden or a farm or your favorite farmers' market stand in exchange for free produce and mentoring about how to create your own garden.
- Grow your own food if possible. Or barter your gardening skills with neighbors or friends who grow food for a selection of free goodies to bring

home. Fresh herbs are pricey to buy but easy to grow, so even if you don't have a garden, pot up a few herb plants.

- Do your research. Ask your veg friends for their best cheap eats ideas and if they have any recipes to swap. It's amazing how many pointers you can get from people who have similar eating practices. Check out cookbooks, YouTube videos, blogs, or join a cooking group or potluck club.

- Cook from scratch! All the recipes in this book are super affordable, and were designed with budgeting in mind.

College dining halls almost always have salad bars, and often will have veggie burgers and vegan-friendly soup options.
—Danielle, Cincinnati, OH

- Consider investing in a slow cooker. It's an inexpensive appliance (you can often find them at yard sales or thrift stores, too), and they're great for cooking staples like beans and soups that you can eat throughout the week rather than spend money eating out.

- Get to know the bulk section in your grocery store. They sell vegan staples like rice, beans, nuts, seeds, and dried fruits and vegetables by the pound at rock-bottom prices.

- Big-box stores like Costco often have great deals on foods like fruits, vegetables, grains, bread, crackers, nut butters, and things like veggie burgers and meat substitutes in the frozen food section.

If you go to a college with very limited vegetarian options, be prepared to have a backup. Cooking for yourself will probably be cheaper than a meal plan anyway. —Mariah, Nashville, TN

VEGANISH HALL: CAMPUS LIFE 101

You made it! Bye-bye, parents, hello, University of Independence. Here's your cheat sheet for life on the outside (of your familiar old homestead):

- Most university dining halls now have at least basic vegan food options. Look for veggie burgers, pastas, soups, salad options. If your dining hall doesn't offer decent options, make friends with the staff; they're your best allies on your quest for plant-based food choices. Make specific requests for the kinds of animal-free foods you'd like to see served, like veggie burgers, tofu swaps, veganish pasta and rice dishes, potatoes, beans, and soups. Rally your carnivore friends to support the requests!

- Find the right meal plan. If available, ask if there's a flexible meal plan that lets you buy your own food from local stores.

- Salad bar. Make your own salads, of course, but also use the salad bar to bulk up your sandwiches with lettuce, tomatoes, cucumbers, carrots, and whatever else looks good to you on a sammie!

- Find the dorm kitchen. Ha, betcha didn't know there was one. Of course I can't guarantee there will be one at your school, but most residence halls do offer a shared kitchen for students who want to cook their own meals. Use it! There's usually a shared microwave, too, if you can't have one in your room.

- Find your people. Join a veg campus club, or start one. Throw a veg-foods party. Seek out your local natural foods store or food co-op. Be part of a community. Learn other locals' veg survive 'n' thrive tips!

- Secure your stash. Store convenient foods in your room, like some energy bars, dried fruit, nuts, pita chips, instant oatmeal and ramen, and microwave popcorn. Try this: Mix a tablespoon of peanut butter into your hot ramen; when it melts, you'll have a hearty peanut sauce that will really fill you up!

- Get your own appliances. If you can, invest in a small fridge and/or microwave for your room if it's allowed. Thrift stores are great for finding cheap appliances.

≈ HERE YOU ARE: ≈ VEGANISH!

Remember that everything great we do in our lives is a work in progress. Set your intention and push forward. Each veganish step takes you further into the momentum of positive change.

> *Since cutting meat out of my diet permanently, I feel a greater confidence in my ability to carve out a lifestyle that can make me proud, contribute positively to others, and bring me emotional fulfillment. I'm excited about how moving toward this lifestyle has brought me new friendships with people who prioritize living a happy, healthy, and kind life. —Evan, Mount Vernon, NY*

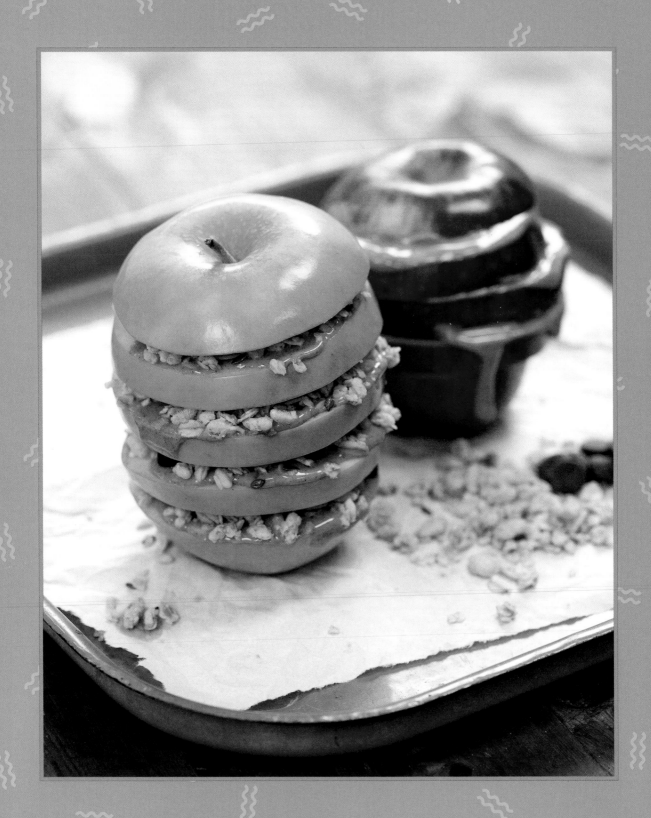

GOT THE MUNCHIES?
THERE'S A SNACK FOR THAT.

I don't know about you, but I consider snacking a crucial component of my day. Snacking keeps me from feeling too hungry between mealtimes and keeps my energy high.

It's so important not to let yourself get too hungry. When your stomach is empty, your body releases ghrelin, the "hunger hormone" that's like an appetite gremlin, signaling you to feed yourself—*now!*—often to the tune of quick, unhealthy foods.

Instead of ignoring that gnawing feeling that hits when you're working long hours, studying, or hanging out, make sure to take a break to rev up your machine. Smart snack choices help you stay focused and keep your energy high until the next meal. There's an entire section devoted to recipes perfect for late nights, group hangs, or just in-between-meal noshing starting on page 229. In the meantime, here are my best tips and tricks for keeping the munchies at bay.

> *I will say that Justin's dark chocolate (vegan) peanut butter cups are better than any Reese's product on the market!*
> —*Laraine, Coshocton, OH*
>
> ~~~~~~
>
> *Kale chips!* —*Zach, Roslyn, NY*

> *Banana ice cream: Freeze two bananas, then throw them in a food processor with a bit of almond milk and any flavoring you want (vanilla, fresh strawberries, peanut butter, cacao powder, etc.) and blend it. It turns into ice cream. Best discovery I've ever made!* —*Cianna, Whittier, CA*

EASY, NO-RECIPE SNACKS

Lazy + healthy snackage = Yum!

- Peanut or almond butter on rice crackers, black bread, celery, or slices of apple
- Popcorn sprinkled with nutritional yeast
- Edamame
- Blue corn chips and salsa/guacamole (hold the sour cream!)
- Hummus with, carrots, celery, or rice crackers
- Nature's candy: Fruit! Apples, pears, grapes (frozen grapes— also great!), plums, berries, bananas, kiwis, melon balls, papaya (drizzle with lime for extra yum!), mango slices, pineapple chunks, pomegranate seeds . . .
- Mashed avocado on toasted bread
- Leftover brown rice or quinoa mixed with nondairy milk, raisins, and cinnamon (my version of rice pudding!)
- Spread some peanut butter on a small tortilla, place a banana on it, sprinkle with some cinnamon or cacao powder, roll it up, and cut it like a sushi roll.
- Spread slices of apple with nut butter like a sandwich, and top with small pieces of bittersweet chocolate. (Fun fact: If it's bitter-sweet chocolate—70% cacao or more—it means there is no milk and is therefore vegan!)
- Almond, soy, or coconut yogurt with some nuts and/or fresh fruit mixed into it

oven or 30 seconds in the microwave to make them extra tasty.

- Kale chips: Make your own by lightly coating pieces of kale with extra-virgin olive oil, then baking in a 350°F oven until crispy, 10 to 15 minutes. Optional: Salt or sprinkle nutritional yeast on top for cheesy flavor.
- Sweet potato fries: Cut a sweet potato into French fry shapes and bake on an oiled baking sheet at 350°F for about 25 minutes. Add salt and pepper and eat hot!
- Couldn't finish that big smoothie? Freeze the leftovers into a popsicle for later!
- A small handful of nuts. Try toasting them for a minute in a toaster

I eat a far more diverse range of foods since going vegan! A fun snack (and healthy dessert!) I like to have is a split banana with warm almond butter on the inside topped with warm mixed berries.
—Sonja, San Jose, CA

Chopped celery and Vegenaise is quick and delicious. Spaghetti with TVP (textured vegetable protein, usually available in the flour aisle of the grocery store) and red sauce is amazing. —Nick, Gainesville, FL

SMOOTHIES 101

I drink a smoothie every day. They are great as either a snack or a meal, and a really satisfying way to get fruits, veggies, protein, and fiber. Especially when they're packed full of frozen kale or broccoli, I get all the nutritional benefits of a hefty serving of vitamin C, fiber, and folate (which your body needs to make and maintain new cells) with a delicious flavor. Boost the protein content of your smoothie by adding vegan protein powder and/or some nut butter. Use the chart on the opposite page to help you build your ideal blend. Just fill your glass three-fourths full with a liquid base, then pour it into your blender and mix and match your favorite options from the Protein, Fruits and/or Veggies, and Bonus Time columns. Blend, pour, and enjoy. Remember:

> Liquid base + protein + 1 or 2 fruits/veggies +
> 1 bonus addition = smoothie nirvana

LIQUID BASE	PROTEIN	FRUITS AND/OR VEGGIES	BONUS TIME
Fill your drinking glass three-fourths full with: Coconut water Nondairy milk, like soy, coconut, or almond Plain ole water A combination of any of the above	Protein powder (I use Vega Sport, but there are lots of brands and even store brands that are fantastic. Just be sure not to use whey protein powder, because that's dairy.) Nut butter Handful of unsalted nuts Tofu	Avocado Frozen broccoli Frozen or fresh kale Frozen or fresh spinach Chard or collard greens Fresh or frozen berries Peeled and frozen banana Cucumber Any fruit	Ground flax seeds Hemp seeds Cacao nibs Agave or stevia to sweeten if needed Chia seeds mixed in after the blend (If you put them in before blending, you'll have pudding, so stir in after!) Nondairy yogurt (Yogurts often have a lot of added sugar, so use sparingly!)

A simple tip for making sure you are getting enough fiber and protein is to make yourself smoothies with chia seeds. Each time I make a smoothie, I add 1 tablespoon of chia seeds, which adds 6 grams of fiber, 3 grams of protein, and 3 grams of omega-3s.
—Madeline, Minneapolis, MN

I love to make a "chocolate shake" for breakfast—3 frozen bananas, a little bit of cacao and carob powder, some water or almond milk, and bam! A chocolate shake for breakfast that your body will actually thank you for. —Laine, Peotone, IL

I make a shake that is extremely healthy and out of this world:

1 frozen banana
½ cup frozen black cherries
4 ice cubes
1 cup vanilla almond milk or coconut milk
½ teaspoon almond extract
1 teaspoon peanut butter
¼ cup edamame energy blend or 3 tablespoons hemp seeds
    or any other portion of nuts
2 scoops of chocolate protein powder

—Hunter, Orlando, FL

≈≈≈ SURPRISE, IT'S VEGAN! ≈≈≈

While I *always* advocate for healthy food choices, it's normal to have cravings for junk food that just can't be ignored once in a while. If you just have to scratch that itch, try to eat a piece of fruit, like an apple, first, to fill your stomach with fiber, and make you feel full fast. That way, you'll be less likely to binge on the less-healthy vegan treats.

Whatever the reason for the craving (bad day at work, hormonal freak-out, study cramming, stress, bad breakup, or Just Because), know that there are vegan choices available to you. So, with a wink and a smile, I offer this list of junk foods that you might be surprised to know are vegan.

DANGEROUS BUT ADMITTEDLY DELISH TREATS	CANDY
Clif Bars	Blow Pops
Doritos Spicy Sweet Chili	Charms lollipops
Oreos	Dots
Original Fritos	Dum-Dums
Kellogg's Unfrosted Pop-Tarts	Fireballs
Ritz Crackers	Goldenberg's Peanut Chews
Betty Crocker Bac~Os Bacon Flavor Bits	Hot Tamales
Pillsbury Crescent Rolls	Hubba Bubba bubblegum
Jell-O Instant Pudding Mix (vanilla, chocolate, lemon, pistachio, and banana crème flavors only)	Jolly Ranchers (lollipops and hard candy)
	Jujubees
Smucker's Marshmallow Ice Cream Topping	Jujyfruits
Cracker Jack	Lemonheads
	Mary Janes (regular and peanut butter kisses)
	Mike and Ike
	Pez
	Smarties (U.S. Brand)
	Sour Patch Kids
	Swedish Fish
	Sweet Tarts
	Twizzlers

For a fuller list of surprise vegan foods, check out the "Accidentally Vegan" page on PETA's website: www.peta.org. But you didn't hear that from me. ☺

HOW NOT TO STARVE
WHEN EATING OUT

As you start to get the hang of your new veganish diet, you'll probably discover that it's easiest to succeed when you are calling the shots and controlling what's in the fridge and kitchen cabinets. For that reason, eating out can be a real roadblock. I'll be honest. Depending on where you live, it can be challenging to find a decent range of veganish food options when you don't make the menu. But don't worry! It's *totally* possible to find what you're looking for. There *are* tasty and amazing food options for you out there. You might have to do a little more work than your carnivore friends to put together a delicious meal at a restaurant, but that's half the fun. Finding what works for you, and where, often leads to surprising and delicious discoveries.

The key is preparation. When possible, try not to wait until you're starving before finding a place to eat. Do your research in advance, if you can. Always try to check out a menu online first so you arrive knowing you will have options to choose from. Decide what you want before you go, and if you're not sure if an item can be veganized, call ahead and ask.

Obviously I want you to have satisfying veganish options wherever you eat, but the reality is that it might not always be possible, particularly if you're attending social functions where you have no say in the menu or restaurant choice. So, if you know your options will be very limited or even nonexistent, do yourself a favor and eat ahead of time. And always keep a bag of nuts, an energy bar, or an easy snack on hand, just in case. If all else fails, just do the best you can and don't make yourself—or everyone else around you—crazy. Veganish is about doing a little better every day, and while I am not advocating throwing up your hands and chowing down on a steak if there isn't a truly vegan option, having a pasta that might not be 100-percent plant-based or settling on a soup that you're not sure is made from veggie stock in order to not starve now and then doesn't make you a "bad" vegan. Remember, labels are not the objective; acting with compassion and thought is the goal here.

I have a "2% rule," meaning that if a dish has a tiny bit of something derived from an animal, I'm not going to drive myself or a waiter crazy about it. I'm not benefitting animals by being an extremist or by being annoying and impossible to please. Remember: Being veganish is about moving *toward* a plant-based diet. It doesn't have to be absolute. That means if I'm at a restaurant, I don't grill the waiter about whether or not there might be egg in the bread. I try to represent the veganish movement as being accessible and flexible. Again, it's about progress, not perfection! (Just to be clear, I'm fully vegan; I'm just suggesting you don't make things impossible for yourself or others.)

～～ VEGANISH-FRIENDLY ～～ RESTAURANT HUNTING

The Internet is your best resource for satisfying your plant-based dining-out desires. The Happy Cow website (www.happycow.net) is a fantastic site for finding veg-friendly restaurants anywhere, and bonus, the user reviews for each restaurant sometimes include recommendations for menu items that diners had modified to be animal-free. Trust your fellow plant-based eaters! Happy Cow is also available as a phone app.

Speaking of phone apps, there are a ton out there, so check out which most appeals to you and refer to it for quick, convenient listings of vegan foods near you.

Another gem is the Yelp app and website. From either Yelp option, search "vegan" or "vegetarian" and your choice of location, and listen to the advice of your compadres! If you're doing a broader restaurant search on Yelp, look for the carrot symbol next to the listings with the message "Vegetarians go nuts for this spot." It's a pretty reliable way to find a restaurant to please everyone in your party.

～～～ HOLD THE BUTTER ～～～
(AND MEAT AND EGGS
AND DAIRY!)

Don't assume that a restaurant's menu is fixed; there's almost always flexibility in how a dish is prepared if you ask politely and with an open mind. I'm always amazed when a waiter replies to my question of "Do you have anything vegan?" with, "Oh yes, the chef makes a wonderful tofu dish!" (Why didn't they put it on their menu in the first place?!) But you'll never know that's an option if you don't put the question out there. By now, most restaurants will have fielded these questions a lot, and will probably have ideas and suggestions. If they don't, go someplace else next time!

If you do end up eating at the place that really doesn't make an effort to accommodate your preferences, help out future veganish diners. Always let restaurateurs know you love their restaurant, but you can't keep coming back if your only options are side dishes, plain salads or pasta, and bread. That should encourage them to add some hearty plant-based dishes or get creative about adapting the existing dishes in the future.

> *I would advise anyone considering veganism or vegetarianism to keep track of what they eat, and closely look at the nutrients, vitamins and minerals they are consuming. The way I do this now is through an application on my phone called MyFitnessPal.*
> *—Laura, Seattle, WA*

∼ VEGANISH RESTAURANT ∼ OPTIONS 101

Here's a quick cheat sheet of vegan foods you'll probably be able to find at most family restaurants. Admittedly, this is not the dynamic stuff that makes eating out a fun adventure, but when your options are limited and your stomach is growling, these are going to be your best bets. Hopefully you won't be stuck with these limited options, but if you are, at least you won't starve!

> *If I know I'm going to end up at a fast food restaurant, I like to pack a sandwich and fruit, and order something like a small order of fries at the restaurant. —Evan, Mount Vernon, NY*

- Vegetable soups (Ask if the soups are made with dairy or meat stock.)
- Bean chili: Hold the cheese
- Pasta with marinara or arrabbiata (spicy tomato) sauce, or with extra-virgin olive oil, veggies, and salt
- Vegetable side dishes like potatoes, steamed or sautéed veggies, corn
- Mixed salad with chickpeas or other beans
- A sandwich with veggies (lettuce, tomato, cucumber, mushrooms, etc.) and hummus or avocado or any other plant-based spread
- At a Mexican place, bean taco/burrito: Ask if the beans are vegan (not made with meat, butter, or lard); hold the cheese and sour cream; add extra salsa, lettuce, and guac. Generally, black beans are vegan while pinto beans are not.
- Pizza or calzone: Ask for one with no meat or cheese, and pile on extra veggies or mushrooms. A lot of pizza joints have nondairy cheese now, so ask! (I've been known to bring my own soy cheese for the proprietor to sprinkle on and put in the oven.)
- At a salad bar, pile on the chickpeas and other beans with all kinds of veggies and opt for the Italian dressing or vinaigrette instead of creamy dressings.
- French fries, though admittedly delicious, are not always vegan (sometimes they're cooked with beef fat), so ask if you're not sure. Baked potato and potato wedges are often better options.

- Many diners offer a vegetable plate, chef's salad (hold the cheese, meat, and/or egg) or salad bar, baked beans, pasta, fruit plate, potatoes, cereal or oatmeal (ask them to make it with nondairy milk, or water if nondairy isn't available).
- Request a "potato scramble" with cubes of potato and vegetables instead of scrambled eggs or omelets. Add tofu if it's available.
- At a steakhouse or seafood restaurant, request a sampler of their veggie sides with a baked potato. Most restaurants will be glad to accommodate. You could also ask your server what other vegans have requested there in the past; your waiter should have a good idea of the best options for non-meat eaters.

 **FAST FOOD**

Your gang wants Mickey D's or other fast food and you're like, *Meh*. You don't want to eat that stuff, and you don't want such limited food options. Guess what—they don't have to be! Fast food restaurants change their menus all the time, and some even offer regional items. To figure out your best bets ahead of time, investigate online by searching "vegan options" and the name of the restaurant chain. I use vegan apps (see page 270) to get an idea of what and where to eat when I'm in a new place; the apps are especially great for fast food restaurant choices. (By the way, I launched a change.org petition asking McDonald's to offer a veggie burger since almost every other fast food joint has one

> The best vegan fast food by far is Taco Bell. So easy to customize being vegan. The fritos burritos with beans instead of beef and no cheese is delicious, filling, and cheap.
> —Nick, Gainesville, FL

and they should have something healthier and more humane on their menu. As of now, they haven't listened to the more than 113,000 of us; if you want to add your voice, go to www .change.org/p/mcdonald-s-it-s-time-for-a-healthy-meatless-option.)

~ EXPLORE THE WORLD, ~ ONE BITE AT A TIME

> *I recommend trying to stick to certain types of restaurants. Vegetarian and vegan, as well as "green" or healthy restaurants, are best. Ethnic food is great, too. Chipotle, Mexican, Indian, Thai, Ethiopian, etc. Also, for chains, look them up online! There's usually a list of vegan items easily available. —Bradley, Philadelphia, PA*

One of the great joys of going vegan is expanding your palate, and experiencing new tastes and foods you might not have considered before. Ethnic restaurants provide a treasure trove of vegan options. Asian cuisines like Chinese, Thai, and Vietnamese use very few dairy ingredients, and most serve tofu in really creative and wonderful ways. Just ask for the options without fish or oyster sauce, or bonito (fish) flakes. Mediterranean restaurants generally offer hearty bean salads or hummus and tabbouleh dishes. Italian food is always *molto delizioso* but ask to hold the cheese and check if the pasta is made with egg (typically the case with fresh pasta, so opt for the dried varieties instead . . . but as I said before, don't make yourself crazy). Indian and Ethiopian restaurants are great bets for a broad selection of animal-free dishes, but ask the waiter if there is any ghee (clarified butter) or paneer (cheese) in the dish if you're eating in an Indian place.

International Cuisine Type	Vegan Staples	Order This!
Chinese	Fresh veggies Noodles Rice Tofu Vegetable dump-lings	Garlic eggplant General Tso's tofu Hot or cold sesame noodles Kung pao tofu Sautéed green beans Veggie stir-fry with garlic sauce Tofu and broccoli in black bean sauce Veggie and/or tofu fried rice (Ask for no egg.) Veggie or tofu chow mein

International Cuisine Type	Vegan Staples	Order This!
Ethiopian	Bread (called injera) Cabbage Collard greens Lentils Potatoes Tomatoes	Timatim fitfit (fresh salad of chopped tomatoes and onion) Yatkilt alitcha (cabbage, potatoes, carrots, and onions) Yeabesha gommen (yummy collard greens) Yemiser wat (spicy lentil stew)
Indian	Bread Cauliflower Curries Onion Potatoes	Aloo gobi (cauliflower and potatoes) Bombay potato Chana masala (savory chickpeas) Chana saag (spinach and chickpeas) Dal (savory dried lentil, pea, or other type of bean) Saag aloo (spinach and potato curry) Tarka dal (lentil stew) Veggie curry Veggie samosa Veggie vindaloo
Italian	Eggplant Mushrooms Pasta Soup Tomatoes Vegetables	Grilled eggplant with marinara sauce Grilled veggies Minestrone soup Pasta e fagioli (little white beans!) soup Pasta primavera Pasta with broccoli and garlic Pizza with marinara sauce and veggies (no cheese) Risotto prepared with veggies, mushrooms, and vegetable stock
Japanese	Fresh and pickled veggies Noodles (udon and soba) Rice	Sushi: —cucumber roll —Japanese pickle roll (typically made with daikon radish) or carrots *(continued)*

International Cuisine Type	Vegan Staples	Order This!
Japanese (continued)	Seaweed Tofu and miso	—avocado roll (often used as tuna substitute; ask for combination sushi roll with avocado and other vegetables) —spinach roll —natto (fermented soy paste) roll —mushroom roll If they have the ingredients, most sushi chefs will prepare custom sushi, such as a California roll without fish. Edamame Shishito peppers Miso soup Seaweed salad Udon or soba noodles or rice with veggies and/or tofu Vegetable gyoza (dumplings)
Mediterranean/ Middle Eastern (Greek, Israeli, Lebanese, Turkish)	Bread (lafa, lavash, pita) Bulgur Cauliflower Chickpeas Couscous Eggplant Leafy greens Lentils Peppers Rice Tomatoes Zucchini	Baba ghanoush (smoky eggplant dip or spread) Dolmas (grape leaves stuffed with rice or bulgur) Falafel plate or falafel sandwich Filfil rumi mahshi (stuffed green peppers) Foul m'damas (fava beans and chickpeas simmered in garlic, lemon juice, and extra-virgin olive oil) Fried artichokes Fried cauliflower Hummus with whole wheat pita bread Lentil soup Mujadarra (lentils and rice) Olives Salad (Greek, Israeli, fattoush, sesame, cabbage, etc.) Sautéed zucchini Tabbouleh

International Cuisine Type	Vegan Staples	Order This!
Mexican	Beans Rice Guacamole Veggies Tofu/sofritas Potato	Bean burrito with lettuce, corn, guacamole, salsa Chips and guac Fajitas with veggies, avocado
Thai	Fresh veggies Tofu Rice Rice noodles Spring rolls Soup Tofu	Stir-fried veggies and/or tofu with curried coconut milk Veggie pad Thai (often made with egg and/or oyster sauce, so specify vegan) Lemongrass soup Sweet sticky mango rice (dessert) Veggie or tofu spring rolls
Vietnamese	Fresh veggies Noodles Rice Sandwiches (banh mi) Soup (pho) Tofu	Veggie spring rolls Veggies and/or tofu with lemongrass Spring noodle salad with tofu Tofu or veggie banh mi Veggie curry Veggie pho

∼∼∼ VEGANIZE THE PARTY ∼∼∼

At a restaurant it's fine to express your preferences; after all, you're a paying customer and the customer's always right, right? But when you're in someone else's home, it's a different story. You don't have the right to demand a special accommodation if the host hasn't thought to provide an option that is in line with your new way of eating. But don't let that make you a party pooper.

If it's a cookout or casual get-together, bring your own veggie burgers or vegan dish. And bring enough to share, because inevitably someone will say, "Ooh, that looks good, can I try it?" Bring a delicious vegan dessert (coconut milk ice cream is one of my go-to's) so that everyone can enjoy the goodness!

If it's a fancier dinner or maybe a family holiday, call the host and tell them you don't want them to waste a steak or piece of fish on you because you're plant-based, and would it be okay if you brought something so they don't have to worry about you. They might just say, "We'll have something for you, not a problem!" If they don't, bring something yummy for yourself.

If it's a hotel event like a wedding or conference, there is usually a vegan option if you simply request it (and it's always helpful to make the request ahead of time, if possible).

ADVENTURE TIME

Vacation! You're on break from the usual grind, and it's time for some fun. Being flung from the comforts of your familiar environment will enliven your mind and nourish your soul. No need to stress on travel food options. Just go prepared.

Travel with whatever veg snacks you love. I always bring nuts and snack bars for a quick fix. You can buy Clif or Luna bars by the carton online pretty inexpensively, or at big-box stores like Costco.

For car, train, and airplane trips, pack leftovers that don't need to be reheated so you don't have to rely on fast food or train/plane food. (I try to save my to-go containers to reuse on these occasions.) No leftovers? No problem! Sandwiches last for hours and require no utensils, making them perfect travel food, and these days airlines offer a vegan meal if you request it ahead of time (and it's usually a lot tastier than what your neighbor will be eating, too!).

When you get to your destination city, stop by a grocery store and grab some soy creamer for coffee, peanut butter, crackers, fruit, precut veggies, microwavable soup (if you have access to a microwave), and small, premade snacks like bean and pasta salads if there's a deli with fresh salad options nearby. And use those vegan-helper apps and websites like Happy Cow and Yelp to find great local food sources.

If you're staying at a hotel, pack instant oatmeal for brekkie. You can use the hotel's coffee maker to boil water for it. Bring a couple travel packs of vegan protein powder just to ensure you're fully recharged for the day's adventures. Ask your hotel or your host if you can borrow a blender, throw in the protein powder with some coconut water or soy milk and fruit, and *voilà*, you have a simple, tasty smoothie. Nerd alert: I also pack a tiny battery-operated handheld blender if I'm camping, which does a great job blending the water and protein powder for a simple smoothie, even if I don't have any other goodies to add.

While you're out exploring and sightseeing, check out the local Indian, Thai, Japanese, and Mexican joints. Wherever you're staying—hotel, hostel, Airbnb, neighbors, campground—see if there are any other vegetarian or vegan guests. Be brave, seek out your fellow vegs, and make it a community adventure to find local food places. And if you find local gems, post reviews online to help future veg travelers! That way you can eat well and pay it forward to other veg-eaters!

Connect with other vegans. It makes it so much easier to tolerate all of those in your life who don't understand your choices when you know you have an entire community of like-minded people who agree with you and support you. If you've gone vegan for ethical reasons, take time to appreciate animals by volunteering at farm sanctuaries or animal shelters. They're a constant reminder of why veganism is so important. Lastly, fall in love with cooking! Experiment with a wide variety of vegan recipes that you find online or in cookbooks. —Danielle, Cincinnati, OH

HOW TO DEAL WITH THE NON-VEGS IN YOUR LIFE

Just when you seem to be happily settling into your new veganish life and feeling good about the changes you've made—not to mention the way you look and feel—something may come along to rain on your parade. You're full of positive energy and generous thoughts, so can that be . . . hostility you're sensing from other people? For making such a compassionate, conscious choice? What the #!&*?

It's a weird thing, but people can get really defensive and angry with you when they hear you're not eating meat. They may act as though you're trying to tell them what *they* should be doing, when it's really all about the best choice *you* have made for *yourself*. It's not uncommon for people who go veganish to feel a tad isolated because they're not eating the same way as everyone else.

That's okay. Leaders and game changers are never ones to go along with the crowd. Be proud that you're different, that you're trying something that feels right. You're taking part in what is going to be a massive cultural shift, and that's a great thing.

If you feel someone is attacking you for your dietary preferences, keep your response simple and kind. I usually say something like, "This way of eating makes sense to me. Nonviolence is important to me, and knowing that my meal didn't cause an animal to suffer feels really good. I'm cool with however anyone chooses to eat, but this veganish thing is working for me." (Because the animal thing is most important to me, I respond like this, but if the health or environmental impact is more important to you, choose what feels right and true, and respond with that.)

If someone wants to know more, I usually offer some thoughts about ethics, the environment, and/or health, depending on what interests them. But

I make sure I am never judgmental, and always caring. Here are a few things I've said in the past when questioned about my decision:

- Ethical: I'm about doing the least harm and the most good, and eating vegan-ish does that. I'm just trying to be thoughtful.
- Environmental: It's so inefficient to cycle crops through animals; it creates so many problems, from water shortages and pollution, to forests being cut down, to global-warming gases, to cesspools of waste. I'd rather just eat from those food crops directly instead of making an animal eat up to ten times as much before I eat their meat. The whole process of animal agriculture just causes too much environmental fallout. And hey, have you seen *Cowspiracy*?
- Health: Too many of my relatives have had heart issues or cancer or diabetes, and I see so many overweight people. It freaks me out. Since there's so much good science saying animal foods really contribute to those problems, I'm opting out of eating them. Besides, I feel really great eating plant-based; my energy is stoked!

Need even more? Borrow from some of these famous folks:

- My body will not be a tomb for other creatures. —*Leonardo da Vinci*
- One should not kill a living being, nor cause it to be killed, nor should one incite another to kill. Do not injure any being, either strong or weak, in the world. —*Buddha*
- There is no fundamental difference between man and animals in their ability to feel pleasure and pain, happiness, and misery. —*Charles Darwin*
- I choose not to make a graveyard of my body for the rotting corpses of dead animals. —*George Bernard Shaw*
- Violence begins with the fork. —*Mahatma Gandhi*

Make sure to believe in yourself and stay confident. You are going to swim against the tide for a while and you may feel like giving up. Surround yourself with people that will support your decision and get you through the rough patches! —Komal, Seattle, WA

~~~~~

If someone asks me at the dinner table why I'm vegan, I like to keep things concise but informative: "I personally don't agree with how animals are treated on factory farms." —Sonja, San Jose, CA

- We cannot have peace among men whose hearts find delight in killing any living creature. —*Rachel Carson*
- Now I can look at you in peace; I don't eat you anymore. —*Franz Kafka*
- I had been a participant in all of the "major" and most of the "minor" civil rights demonstrations of the early sixties. Under the leadership of Dr. King, I became totally committed to nonviolence, and I was convinced that nonviolence meant opposition to killing in any form. I felt the commandment Thou Shalt Not Kill applied to human beings not only in their dealings with each other—war, lynching, assassination, murder, and the like—but in their practice of killing animals for food and sport. Animals and humans suffer and die alike. Violence causes the same pain, the same spilling of blood, the same stench of death, the same arrogant, cruel, and brutal taking of life. —*Dick Gregory (civil rights activist)*
- I became a vegetarian after realizing that animals feel afraid, cold, hungry, and unhappy like we do. I feel very deeply about vegetarianism and the animal kingdom. It was my dog Boycott who led me to question the right of humans to eat other sentient beings. —*Cesar Chavez*

> *My immediate family is very supportive of my life to live a vegan lifestyle. When explaining my lifestyle choice to my family or friends, I first talk about what is most important to me, which is animals. I am vegan for the animals, and health benefits come along with it. I am not vegan for my health; I am healthy because I am vegan. I do point out the health benefits to most people, because I know that is how they can understand my choice.*
> —*Tess, Walnut Creek, CA*

∼∼ VEGAN POLICE: NO ONE'S ∼∼ FAVORITE FRIEND

> *Come and talk to me about it. We can eat a few meals together and I will be around to answer any questions that you have.* —*Brianna, Philadelphia, PA*

Vegans sometimes talk about feeling alienated, but they don't always realize that they can *become* alienating just by talking about it *too much*. When you are passionate about your choice and let everyone you know how *right* that decision feels, the people around you may feel you are judging them for not making that same choice. Not cool. Remember, this is a choice you've made for yourself, but you got there in your own time and in your own way. No one bullied you into it or belittled you for past behavior, but you got there nonetheless. Trust that others will find their way as well.

I'm thrilled to be part of a conscious, forward-thinking community of people trying to make a positive difference, but I believe it's important to provide an open, nonjudgmental welcome mat for everyone else. They should feel invited to step into the veganish life without feeling attacked or dismissed; everyone has their own path and their own time line. I understand why meat eaters sometimes avoid the topic of plant-based diets with vegans who are too strident about it. When I was new to all of this, if someone approached me with a dogmatic point of view, I stubbornly refused to consider their opinions. I can think for myself, thank you very much! And I trust you can, too. Just be chill about it. Follow your own heart. Find your way, and if someone wants help, assist them in any way you can. Lead by example, not by condescension or ridicule.

> If someone doesn't have a positive opinion of vegetarianism or veganism, that's fine, because it only matters that you find contentment in your decision. —Evan, Mount Vernon, NY

> I think the most effective way to speak to anyone who loves you but doesn't eat the same way is to emphasize how important animal rights are to you, and how much it hurts you to see meat on the table or in the store, instead of putting blame on them. They get defensive. They just do. . . . When someone makes a vegan meal or side for me at their party, I rave. People like compliments. They like to be appreciated. They like to feel like they did something good. And that, more than chiding, will make them want to do it more. —Emily, Los Angeles, CA

DEALING AND DATING: ASK KATHY

~~~~~~

As you transition to a veganish lifestyle, lots of new issues will come up with the people in your life who are not veg. Here are some of the common ones, with my thoughts on how to deal.

What advice do you have for talking to my family about going veg if they're committed carnivores?

Just like you don't want anyone telling you what you "should" or "shouldn't" do, you're better off just authentically sharing your reasons (if asked, that is) about why you're eating differently these days. If someone is worried or concerned about the health aspect of a veganish diet, they can either read this book, my book *Veganist*, or look in the Resources (pages 268-72) section of this book for a deeper dive.

Let them know that even though they may feel differently about food choices, you'd love their support and goodwill; tell them no one likes to feel dismissed or invalidated. Keep it simple.

What can I do to help someone—a family member, friend, or someone I'm dating—see how important this is to me?

You can share a video that moved you. You can tell your story, how and why something affected you and how you've changed because of it. Bear in mind that the goal is not to convert anyone, but rather to help them understand why *you* are the way you are. The goal is to feed and stoke a connection, as it's in connectedness with someone that new ideas are welcomed.

What should I do if someone really important to me is completely closed to a conversation about moving toward a plant-based diet?

Well, hopefully whomever you're choosing to be around cares enough about you to try to understand your worldview. There's nothing more important to a rela-

(continued)

tionship—any kind of relationship—than for both parties to feel witnessed, understood, and appreciated for who they are. Even if there are differences of opinion, you can still respect and enjoy each other.

If, on the other hand, someone is teasing you or flat out insulting you, you might do well to rethink where you want to put your precious energy and time. Bullying is not cool. You could say, "Hey, this stuff is really important to me. I get that you're not into it, but let's try to communicate to each other kindly and respectfully."

Remember: It's not your job to convert anyone; your job is to stay true to yourself.

How do I tell someone I'm dating that ultimately I want to be with someone who is also veganish?

It's never okay (and it never works) to ask someone to change their beliefs so that they are more aligned with ours. We all believe what we believe; none of us has control over our authentic feelings. But we *can* articulate what matters to us and why, and then let another person know what our triggers are. For instance, you could say, "When I see meat on the plate, what I really see is an animal who suffered and died. I find it distressing, so I'm just letting you know that I might tear up or wince or tune out if you're eating chicken or whatever in front of me. It's not my business to tell you what or what not to eat, but I want to stay connected with you, so I just have to let you know that." Then it's up to him or her to decide what to do with that information.

(And just FYI, if you're looking to date someone who is veganish, join an animal rights organization like PETA, the Humane Society of the United States, Farm Sanctuary, or Mercy for Animals to meet like-minded people. Or try a Meetup or explore some veg-oriented online dating sites!)

What if my partner/friend has seen the videos of what happens to animals and has read the environmental and health stuff but *still* isn't interested in leaning toward becoming veganish?

Let's be honest, a lot of this information—especially the slaughterhouse videos—is pretty shocking. People deal with trauma or potential change in very different ways: They go numb, they protect themselves, they rationalize. I took in the information very slowly and incrementally. Readiness is a very personal thing, so be patient. But also respect yourself enough to choose to be around people who are open-minded and interested in personal growth.

What do I say to someone who is totally convinced that animal protein is the only way to go?

Arguing the issue rarely wins anyone over. And, in fact, it may cause them to dig in even more than before. Have you ever noticed that the more you push, the more someone resists? You'd be better off saving your energy than trying to convince someone to see things your way. Find the common ground between you and focus on what keeps you connected; accept the person for who he or she is. Then decide whether you're really getting enough from the relationship to keep it going despite some fundamental differences in your belief systems.

Ultimately you want to be with someone you can totally be yourself around; you don't want to have to self-edit all the time. If you don't have enough of that connection, the relationship probably isn't a solid and rewarding one. For either of you. You can say something like, "Hey, I respect what's important to you, and I also know myself well enough to identify what makes me happy and comfortable. I'm afraid we're not on the same page about too many things."

7

TEAM VEGANISH TEEN

If you're under the age of eighteen, this chapter is for you. It will help you deal with issues you'll come up against that might be different from those of your slightly older veganish friends, who are out on their own.

When you're living at home with your parents or other guardians, you might not have as much say as you'd like in what's for dinner every night. Don't get frustrated. There are solutions—for dinner, and breakfast, and lunch, too! Let's break it down by mealtimes.

BREAKFAST ON THE GO

If scrambled eggs and bacon—or even a toaster waffle—are the most common items on your home breakfast menu, how do you avoid skipping the most important meal of the day without undoing all your good veganish work? A little bit of advance planning will go a long way. At night before you turn in, make a breakfast parfait in a mason jar, then simply grab 'n' go on your way out the door. (And don't be surprised if you get a lot of oohs and ahhs for your yummy-looking breakfast jar!)

MASON JAR BREKKIE

1 part base + 1 part liquid + 1 part topping + 1 tablespoon bonus booster = One fab way to start the day

BASE	LIQUID	TOPPING	BONUS
Raw rolled oats	Nut milk	Frozen berries	Seeds—chia, flax, sesame, pumpkin
Cooked quinoa	Nondairy yogurt	Sliced banana	Goji berries
Cooked brown rice		Fresh fruit in season	Cacao nibs
Granola		Fruit jam	Agave nectar
Muesli			

SCHOOL LUNCH

Lunchtime can be one of the biggest obstacles when you're trying to go veganish. Many school cafeterias offer salads, veggie sides, and veggie burgers, but these options are usually pretty limited and can get monotonous real fast. If your school doesn't offer a good range of plant-based foods, speak up! Petition your principal and school cafeteria manager for animal-free food options, and make specific suggestions for foods you'd like to see added that would appeal to everyone, regardless of their dietary preference. Ask them to offer oatmeal or bran cereal and soy milk for breakfast; cheese-less (or nondairy cheese) pizza piled with veggies, hummus wraps, or black bean burritos for lunch. Here's a good example of how one teen did it: www.vrg.org/teen/high_school_cafeteria.php.

But the truth is, you'll have better options and more belly satisfaction if you pack your own lunch. Yeah, geek alert! Display that healthy homemade lunch with pride . . . and expect a lot of envious glances from everyone else eating that gross-looking cafeteria meat mush.

BUILD YOUR OWN SANDWICH OR WRAP

BREAD	BASE	VEGGIE	FRUIT	SPREAD
Whole-grain bread	Nut butter	Lettuce	Apple	Black bean dip
Pita	Hummus	Spinach	Banana	Balsamic dressing
Lavash	Avocado	Kale	Pear	Tahini
Tortilla	Baked tofu	Sprouts		Cashew cheese
Bagel	Baked (or microwaved) sweet potato	Cucumber		Vegan cream cheese
Crackers	Sautéed mushrooms	Tomato		Vegan mayo
English muffin	Falafel	Carrot		Guacamole
	Baked eggplant	Olives		Cranberry sauce
	Roasted zucchini	Pickle		Fruit spread (jam, jelly, chutney)
	Veggie meat (like Tofurky brand)	Onion		
	Veggie cheese slice			
	Refried beans			

Don't limit yourself to sandwiches just because they are the traditional lunch box filler. Bring whatever appeals to you and will give you enough energy to get through the day. Maybe you'd rather eat a few snacks throughout the day than one big heavy meal; it's all good. Keep a few resealable (and reusable!) plastic sandwich bags of goodies in your backpack for easy access between classes.

- Salad: leafy greens, quinoa, beans, veggies, maybe with a veggie burger crumbled over it and topped with your favorite nondairy dressing
- Any kind of mixed bean salad
- Fruit
- Veggie or fruit crisps (like sweet potato, kale, or apple chips)
- Dried fruit or veggies
- Celery with peanut butter or almond butter
- Raw veggies like carrots, celery, or cucumber slices with hummus
- Vegan energy bars like Clif or Luna
- A thermos container of hot soup or veggie chili
- Cold pasta bowl or grain bowl with your favorite meatless sauce
- Nuts and seeds
- Nondairy yogurt
- Pack leftovers. Leftovers ROCK.

Being vegan has kept my weight even with no fluctuating. Being a teenager, with all the hormones happening, you lose control sometimes. But my vegan diet has kept me physically able and I very rarely get tired during the day. I would say I have more energy than my friends the majority of the time. —Heather, Los Angeles, CA

DINNER

If you're the lone veganish eater at the table and other family members don't feel like preparing meatless options, how about volunteering to cook for yourself? It's quick and easy to learn to make things like grains, beans, salads, and veggie stir-fries. Try some of the recipes at the back of this book. They were designed specifically for people who are new to cooking, and they're great starter recipes to make on your own or with family. Taking charge of your own meals by learning to cook (starting with basics, and seeing if you want to try more advanced dishes over time) will be one of the best tools you could ever give yourself to succeed in adopting a plant-based diet. (But if you don't like to cook, no worries! As I'm sure you've discovered, there are many simple and delicious ways to eat veganish without making like a master chef.)

> Compromises are the key to dining with a split family. —Komal, Seattle, WA
>
> At my house, I usually cook something vegan for everyone or my family makes sure there are things I can eat, too. For example, if they're having beef tacos, they make me potato tacos.
> —Cianna, Whittier, CA

If your family members are committed carnivores, ask whoever is cooking to make a couple of nonmeat side dishes. If meat is used in a dish that's not a main, like bacon or chicken tossed in a salad, or eggs in a pasta or rice dish, ask for it to be prepared with the meat on the side. Add some easy-to-prepare quinoa, rice, beans, and a salad to your side dishes, and you're set for a meal as complete as the others sitting at the table. And maybe, if your family is game, you can try Meatless Monday dinner at your home. If you guys are going out to dinner as a family, request that it's a place where everyone—veg or carnivore—will be able to eat well. As long as you make requests instead of demands, and make it clear you are not judging their choices, it's likely your family will be supportive, and hopefully enticed to try some vegan meals, too!

> Out of my five siblings, only two eat meat. Family dinners can be a little complicated when everybody comes home, but for the most part there is a main dish that we all can eat, and sometimes meat on the side for those that eat it. —Lydia, Hartland, ME

If a full vegan meal seems like too big a step for your family, try veganizing one dish at time. Remember those easy swaps from chapter 3? Ask your family to give those a try. Use vegetable broth in risottos, veg mayo instead of egg mayo, extra-virgin olive oil instead of butter. These swaps will be tasty for everyone, and make a lot of "regular" foods more accessible to you. And the more you eat "regular" foods, the harder you'll study. Yeah, sure, make that case. ;)

GRANDMA IS REALLY, REALLY WORRIED YOU'RE NOT GETTING ENOUGH PROTEIN, CALCIUM, AND IRON

It's going to happen. Someone you know and love—Mom or Dad, Grandma or Grandpa, your second cousin once removed, your aunt's seemingly cool new boyfriend or girlfriend, your best friend's stepmom, etc.—is going to look at you skeptically and say, "But . . . where are you getting your protein? And calcium? And iron? Is this really a healthy decision?"

In chapter 6, I gave a few ideas for responding to people about your new food choices. But if you are *so* done trying to explain yourself to the Adults in Your Life, or feel confused and tongue-tied about what to say, I'm going to do you a favor. I'm going to tell them for you.

Here's a letter from me to them. Show it to them, send it to them, read it to them, whatever feels most comfortable to you. You can download a PDF from my website, KathyFreston .com, in the section that is devoted to this book. Now go back to your vegan food blogs or Pinterest pages and let *me* take care of talking to the folks. I got this.

Dear Mom/Dad, Aunt/Uncle, Grandma/Grandpa, Family Friend, Committed Carnivore:

> *Wow, your young person wants to go veganish. Congrats! They've obviously been nurtured with great values and a compassionate heart, and now they'd like to reflect that upbringing in their food choices. You must be so proud.*
> *But I know you're also worried. You wonder if vegans and vegetarians get enough protein and iron, along with other essential vitamins and minerals. You're concerned because you've heard that an animal-free diet isn't cost effective. I'd like to allay your concerns and tell you about what a healthy, safe, and effective choice your young person is making.*

First, let me tell you what the medical community has to say. When the esteemed Academy of Nutrition and Dietetics surveyed all the studies on food and health, they concluded: (1) that a vegetarian or vegan diet is as healthy as one that includes meat and, more important, that (2) "vegetarians have been reported to have lower body mass indices than non-vegetarians, as well as lower rates of death from ischemic heart disease, lower blood cholesterol levels, lower blood pressure, and lower rates of hypertension, type 2 diabetes, and prostate and colon cancer."

*How's this for a nice surprise: Since veganish young people skip the cholesterol and fat that's found in animal foods and get more of that important fiber, which is absent in animal foods, they actually tend to have **better** nutrition than their peers. People who eat plant-based diets tend to eat less junk food, and their diets naturally lean toward nutrient-rich foods. Here's how a veganish young person can satisfy his/her primary nutritional needs:*

Protein: *Whole grains, vegetables, beans, nuts, and nondairy milks like almond or soy milks are all good sources of protein, as are healthy meat alternatives like tofu and tempeh, which are made with soybeans, and seitan, which is made with wheat. Worried about soy? Don't. For thousands of years, people in China and Japan lived on a diet rich with soy, and they didn't see much cancer or heart disease or obesity until the Western diet came in and changed the food landscape.*

Calcium: *Green leafy vegetables, broccoli, beans and legumes, and almonds all deliver calcium, or they can drink fortified orange juice. But I'd be careful with juice; all the fiber is removed so it's like drinking sugary soda. Real, whole foods are best.*

Iron: *Greens and beans give them optimal amounts of iron, and vitamin-C-rich foods like citrus actually enhance the absorption of iron when consumed in the same meal.*

*The one crucial nutrient not in a vegan diet is vitamin B12, so it's important they take a supplement with B12 daily. It's the best and most effective weapon to guarantee that non-meat eaters get the **complete** nutritional content they. need.*

I want to assure you that your young person's choice to move away from animal foods is not an attack on you or your lifestyle. It's a personal choice that comes from research, investigation, and thoughtful decision making. It doesn't mean he or she thinks **you** need to make that choice. They've just made the decision that feels right in **their** hearts. And it's an entirely safe and healthy diet that will reward them over time with increased energy, optimal weight, and reduced risk of obesity, diabetes, heart disease, and cancer.

I promise that communal meals don't have to be difficult. I suggest you start by providing simple substitutions. When it's taco night, offer your non-meat eater black bean or lentil fillings instead. Both are cheap and easy to make and will honor your child's wishes without much effort on your part. Meat alternatives like veggie burgers, sausages, meatless crumbles, and meatballs are easy to find in your grocery store's frozen food aisle, and actually are much less expensive than animal meat. Don't you generally have a salad and/or a vegetarian side dish or two at family meals already? A collection of healthy side dishes is a perfectly fine way for a veganish eater to make a complete meal if you skip the butter and cheese. Making staples like beans and some kind of cooked whole grain (brown rice, millet, quinoa, buckwheat; or you can buy a big bag of mixed grains and cook them all together) available as a nonvegan alternative to a meal is a cheap and nutritious way to respect your child's wishes without having to become a short-order cook. Or why not give your young person the ingredients and tools to make those staples for themselves? Try cooking some meat-free dishes together! This book has some terrific and simple recipes that were specifically designed for young people to make for themselves, or with their family and friends. If you're game to experiment with more vegan food, perhaps consider adopting Meatless Monday in your household. You'll be amazed by the abundance of delicious, healthy, nutritious, and affordable options that everyone in the household will like and look forward to.

Thank you for supporting your dear young person and helping them lean into a veganish diet. And don't worry: They **will** get their protein, calcium, and iron!

Love and good health,
Kathy Freston

THE DOCTOR IS IN

~~~~~~

Just so that you can hear it directly from a doctor, I've consulted with Dr. Neal Barnard on your behalf so that any questions you may have are answered here. Dr. Barnard is an adjunct associate professor of medicine at the George Washington University School of Medicine and Health Sciences, a Life Member of the American Medical Association, and a member of the American Diabetes Association. You can give this to your parent or guardian, or just study it for your own benefit!

How can I tell if a young person is well nourished or not?

The first thing to understand is that young people following vegan diets are usually *better* nourished than their meat-eating friends. If that sounds surprising, it's important to remember that vegetables, fruits, and other plant-based foods are nutrient-rich. Meats have some nutrients but are lacking in others, like vitamin C, fiber, and healthy complex carbohydrates.

That said, it's good to be sure that your young one is getting adequate nutrition, and it's not easy to tell how well nourished a child or teen is based on outward appearances. Sometimes blood tests can help, showing if someone is anemic, for example. And, of course, you can check to be sure that a child's weight is in the normal range.

The best thing to do is to ensure that youngsters' meals include the healthy four food groups—vegetables, fruits, whole grains, and legumes (beans, peas, and lentils)—and that they also have a reliable source of vitamin B12, such as a daily multivitamin. That way, they will get the nutrition they need.

Is it true that there are lots of good sources of calcium without milk?

Yes, the best are green vegetables. Broccoli, kale, collards, and many others are loaded with calcium. Beans are, too. So when you think calcium, think greens and beans.

(continued)

My kid's version of going vegetarian seems to be just subsisting on French fries and potato chips instead of meat and dairy. How can I be supportive but make sure he's getting balanced nutrition?

Keep those four healthy food groups—vegetables, fruits, whole grains, and legumes (beans, peas, and lentils)—in mind as you stock your kitchen shelves, and favor the foods you know your young one likes. If apples, oranges, bananas, and other healthy foods are on hand, your child is likely to eat them. And make things "snack-size." Cut up a cantaloupe or melon into bite-size pieces, and keep them in a bowl in the refrigerator. It will soon disappear!

Needless to say, it's best if parents go plant-based, too. That way, you'll not only get the benefits of a healthy diet, you will also be familiar with the many healthful and tasty foods you'll want your child to eat. As you learn how to make the world's best veggie pizza, an irresistible chili, a spicy bean burrito, and killer lasagna, your children will want them, too.

Will a vegan diet stunt a young person's growth? What developmental concerns should a parent have?

Certainly not! In research studies, children following plant-based diets reach the same height as their meat-eating friends and are much less likely to become overweight as adults.

What do I need to know about their diet when my kid hits puberty? Do supplements need to change?

Everything stays the same, there's just more of it. That is, portion sizes naturally grow as the young person's energy needs increase.

What's the best way to make sure they get B12?

Many foods are fortified with vitamin B12. It is often added to soy milk, breakfast cereals, and other products. However, to make sure your young one is getting the right amount of B12, I recommend a supplement. The simplest is a daily multivitamin. All common brands provide more than enough B12.

You will also see supplements that contain B12 alone, without the other vitamins, and they are fine, too. You'll notice that many brands have surprisingly large quantities—1,000 micrograms or more—which is far more than you need. Teenagers actually only need 2.4 micrograms of B12 per day (same as adults), and younger children need slightly less than that. But there is no danger from high doses of vitamin B12.

Exactly which foods should they be eating to replace the protein and iron in meat, and how will those foods affect their health? For example, soy-based foods are common substitutes, but there are some concerns about overconsumption of soy as well as preservatives in those foods since they are rather processed and mostly from the frozen section.

Protein is always the first thing parents worry about, but it turns out to be a complete nonissue. Beans, grains, vegetables, and even fruit all have protein, and as long as a child is getting a variety of these foods, there will be enough protein in his or her diet—even if she or he is a very athletic child.

For iron, "greens and beans" is again the key refrain just as it was for providing calcium. Green leafy vegetables and beans are iron rich.

By the way, if you are worried about soy products, it's good to think about a couple of things: First, soy foods like soy burgers and soy bacon are far healthier than the animal-derived versions of these products, because they have no cholesterol, very little fat, and are loaded with essential fiber. Second, some rather paranoid-sounding websites have suggested that people consuming soy products might have fertility problems or a higher cancer risk. It turns out that soy does not cause fertility problems, and if anything, it helps prevent cancer. A recent large study by the National Institutes of Health showed that women consuming the most soy had about a 40 percent *reduction* in their risk of developing breast cancer.

Soy products are optional, and you can skip them, if you like. But they are handy, tasty, and appear to reduce cancer risk.

(continued)

I'm worried my child is getting *too thin*. Is there enough healthy fat in a vegan diet?

Be a bit careful about deciding that your child is too thin, because nowadays, we are comparing our children with other kids who are getting more and more overweight. If your pediatrician has not determined that your child's weight is an issue, you'd be smart to forget about it.

That said, if a child needs more calories, nuts and nut butters are especially concentrated in calories, and there are plenty of calories in many nondairy milks, too.

How would a vegan diet affect someone with Crohn's disease?

Many people with Crohn's disease feel much better when they switch to a vegan diet. The credit may go to the fiber in vegetables, fruits, and beans, or to the absence of dairy products. In fact, some researchers suspect that the disease was transmitted to humans from a microbe found in cow's milk. That theory is still under investigation, but we do know that a plant-based diet is often helpful for people with Crohn's.

Is there an appropriate age when a young person can reliably make this choice?

A vegan diet is a good choice at any age. And it's a good thing for their parents to begin, too. It helps everyone stay lean and healthy.

CHLOE FALKENHEIM

~~~~~~

NAME: Chloe Falkenheim
AGE: 18
LOCATION: Arlington, VA

At age 18, dynamo Chloe Falkenheim is already a seasoned vegan activist. As a high school student she founded Vegetarian and Vegan Youth (www.VegYouth. com), a nonprofit network of student leaders and youth, which is now one of the preeminent resources for veg-leaning young people. Her club, Students Advocating Vegetarian Eating (SAVE), convinced her school to add falafel, bean wraps, couscous salad, and tomato sauce (instead of meat sauce) to the school menu and they designed a labeling system to facilitate eating vegetarian and vegan in the cafeteria. She also brought speakers to talk to 500 students about factory farming and the benefits of vegetarianism and successfully advocated adding plant-based nutrition to the Yorktown High School teachers' health curriculum. She started a school garden through the Roots and Shoots club at her high school that delivered foods such as basil and broccoli to the cafeteria to be included in the school's meals.

What inspired you to go vegan?

What's more powerful for me is what inspires me to *stay* vegan. I stay vegan because I know eating plant-based is one of the best things one can do to help the animals, the environment, and their own personal health and well-being.

What are your favorite vegan foods?

Not in any particular order, but I love chocolate, spinach, mangoes, strawberries, blueberries, raspberries, mac and vegan cheese, and vegan cookie dough.

(continued)

Restaurant tips?

Don't be afraid to ask for something off the menu. Usually chefs are totally willing to make something new for you! Also, get your friends and family to go to vegetarian/vegan restaurants as much as possible, or to try some good veg options wherever they are. That'll get your friends to see how delicious vegan food is, and will also support vegan businesses!

Any favorite recipes or snack ideas to share?

I love green smoothies. Mix nondairy milk with spinach, bananas, and flax seeds (for omega-3s) for a basic, superhealthy smoothie. You can make a million variations of this by changing the greens, nondairy milk, and fruits. I also really love peanut butter and banana sandwiches with cookies inside as a dessert-like snack.

What advice do you have for people who are trying to move to a plant-based diet?

Go at it slowly, and make gradual changes. Think of yourself as enhancing rather than replacing. Focus more on eating as many plant-based foods as possible and don't worry about being perfect. Think of it as a broader issue than just doing what's good for yourself; it's about that, but it's also good all around, for everyone.

For teens who live at home with nonvegetarians, show your family how great it is to be vegan by cooking for them, and helping them make vegan alternatives to traditional family meals. Eating veg within a nonveg home is easy when you make a plant-based version of the one that's already on the stove. Just keep persisting despite obstacles; it's so worth it!

〜〜〜 YOU EAT WHAT? 〜〜〜

As with so many things these days, the way we eat isn't black and white, all or nothing. As you become more attuned to the nuances of your own diet, and what you will or won't put on your plate, you may run into others who define the way *they* like to eat with one of these terms:

CARNIVORE: Technically it means animals that eat only meat, but it's also slang for humans who love and eat a lot of meat.

FLEXITARIAN: Primarily eats plant-based foods with the occasional inclusion of animal products.

MACROBIOTIC: Eats grains as a staple food, along with legumes, local in-season vegetables, seaweed, some fruit (mostly cooked); avoids the use of highly processed foods. Sometimes, a small amount of fish is eaten.

OMNIVORE: Eats both plants and animals.

PALEO: Eats meat, fish, eggs, vegetables, limited fruits, and nuts, while avoiding processed foods, sugar, soft drinks, grains, most dairy products, and legumes (beans).

PESCATARIAN: Abstains from eating animal flesh, but does eat fish regularly.

RAW: Eats unprocessed plant-based foods that have not been heated between 104 and 120°F (40 and 49°C) in an effort to retain the complete nutritional value of foods.

VEGAN: Eats anything that doesn't come from an animal.

VEGETARIAN: This is an umbrella term for many types of people who don't eat animal flesh or fish, with these qualifiers:

> **LACTO VEGETARIAN:** Doesn't eat animal flesh, fish, or eggs, but does eat dairy products.
>
> **LACTO-OVO VEGETARIAN:** Doesn't eat animal flesh or fish, but does eat dairy and eggs.
>
> **OVO VEGETARIAN:** Doesn't eat any animal foods except eggs.

VEGANISH: My favorite! Someone whose intention is to steer clear of animal foods altogether, but realizes it's a process and does the best they can, without judgment toward others.

GO FORTH AND THRIVE

You probably still have questions, and things will come up as you go forward. Just remember, this is about you *moving forward*; it's not about being perfect or having it all figured out at once. It took me a while to find my footing in the vegan world, to get comfortable and happy with my new way of eating. What carried me through this process was deciding that I was just going to stay awake and aware and do the best I can, and remain committed to nudging myself forward, even if I occasionally slipped backward. Being mellow about it allowed me to transition into the healthy, happy vegan gal I am today.

On my journey to becoming vegan, I was lucky to have fellow travelers answer my questions. In honor of them, I'd like to do the same for you, and answer some of the common questions and issues that come up when making the transition away from animal foods and embracing a plant-based diet.

What's the deal with ethically produced meat and dairy food labels, like "humanely raised," "free range," "grass-fed," "organic"?

There are a lot of misleading labels in the food industry, and many "organic" companies are simply factory farms with a good PR team.

"Humanely raised" means different things to different manufacturers of animal foods. For example, for a broiler chicken, a "free range" label can mean there is one tiny little doorway in a massively huge "barn" that houses thousands of hens or chickens. There's no way that a chicken is going to navigate her way all the way over to that door because her body is way too heavy for her legs to support. (Almost all birds raised for food are genetic hybrids and grow three times as fast with a third of the feed as the birds of yesteryear; because they're intensively bred for their meat, they're ridiculously heavy and can only walk a few labored steps at a time. Check out the organization Farm Forward to learn more on this.) "Grass-fed" usually just means that the cows or chickens are out in a pasture and may have been fed a healthier diet. (But only if the label says *100%* grass-fed; otherwise they may have only experienced the outdoors for a very short time relative to living out their lives in a shed.) "Pasture-raised" or "grass-fed" animals may live their short lives in nicer, more pastoral places than their factory farm counterparts (and some farms do better jobs at this than others), but the animals still meet their ends in the same slaughterhouses where they can hear and smell everything that's happening around them; their suffering is as immeasurably horrible as non-grass-fed or so-called free-range animals. There are no wonderful, "humane," "free range," or "organic" slaughterhouses.

Just as important, there's simply not enough land on the planet to support "humane" animal agriculture on the scale at which we are consuming meat. The answer is not to move to eating humanely sourced meat, but rather to reduce the amount we consume, or eliminate meat entirely.

I think the central question to ask about "humanely" produced animal foods is, "If I were that animal, would I consider the slaughterhouse kill floor humane?" Animals may not be able to anticipate their end in the same conscious way that we do, but all we have to do is look at their survival instinct to appreciate that all creatures cling to life with absolute intensity. When threatened, they fight for life. You can see it in their eyes, like they're begging for help. You can see them shaking and squirming and trying to get away. In the end, I believe you have to ask yourself: Is that really okay with me; is their suffering worth that glass of milk or piece of chicken?

As for "organic" dairy products, be aware that on virtually all farms, organic or otherwise, calves are taken from their mothers soon after birth so that humans can take the milk meant for the calves. This is a wrenching process; there are so many testimonials about calves screaming and mother cows bellowing as they are torn apart from each other. Male calves are either confined to veal crates to be slaughtered after just weeks of life (there would be virtually no veal industry if it wasn't for the dairy industry's need to get rid of male calves) or they're raised for beef, while the female calves are sent to replace old, depleted dairy cows. Dairy cows are killed generally at just four to five years old, a fraction of their natural life span, when their production declines.

At the slaughterhouse, many cows are still conscious when their throats are slit and they are dismembered. This happens on organic dairy farms as well as regular factory farms. Sadly, drinking any kind of dairy milk, organic or not, supports the abuse and death of these gentle animals. And many organic farms exploit major loopholes to keep cows in factory farming conditions while still enjoying the price premium that an "organic" label brings. Again, whether or not you choose to consume these foods comes down to the same deeply personal question: Is that all right with me?

HIGH-PROTEIN DIETS DON'T WORK LONG TERM

Let's go deep into insanely popular high-animal-protein, low-carb diet, because you're going to run into people who are zealots about it, and you may wonder if in fact this way of eating is as great as they say it is. It's *not*.

It's bad for your body. This is what Dr. James W. Anderson, professor of medicine and clinical nutrition at the University of Kentucky, said about a high-animal-protein diet: "People lose weight, at least in the short term. . . . But this is absolutely the worst diet you could imagine for long-term obesity, heart disease, and some forms of cancer." In fact, when *U.S. News and World Report* did its annual Best Diets Rankings in 2015, Paleo came up dead last, based on input from a panel of health experts. These experts—doctors and nutritional scientists from prestigious organizations all over the country—assessed thirty-five different diets based on nutrition, safety, ease of adherence, weight-loss friendliness, and protectiveness against diabetes and heart disease. They concluded that Paleo is too high in fat, and shuns entire food groups that are perfectly healthy.

Dr. Dean Ornish is a clinical professor of medicine at the University of California, San Francisco, and the founder of the Preventive Medicine Research Institute. In an excellent piece that appeared in *The New York Times* (google Dean Ornish, *The Myth of High-Protein Diets*), Dr. Ornish explains it this way: "Animal protein increases IGF-1, an insulin-like growth hormone, and chronic inflammation, an underlying factor in many chronic diseases. Also, red meat is high in Neu5Gc, a

(continued)

tumor-forming sugar that is linked to chronic inflammation and an increased risk of cancer." He writes, "Research shows that animal protein may significantly increase the risk of premature mortality from all causes, among them cardiovascular disease, cancer, and type 2 diabetes. Heavy consumption of saturated fat and trans fats may double the risk of developing Alzheimer's disease."

So you'll see people proselytizing for the high-protein, low-carb diet (meaning lots of animal foods and no grains), but unfortunately for them, bad things are likely to go on in their bodies later in life.

(Oh, and after a while on a high-animal-protein diet, your body gives off a weird pungent smell and your breath gets skanky, too. So there's that.)

I really don't want to give up eggs! What if they're cage-free?

"Cage-free" is a label that's been manufactured by the egg industry itself. It serves them well, but the lines are very blurred as to what "cage-free" or "free-range" actually means. The cold truth is that no matter how they are labeled, egg-laying hens are the single worst-treated animals on the planet. There are no laws to protect them. You can basically kick them, throw them, chop their beaks off, chop their toes off. They live in supertight confines, they contract diseases, and they are in pain. It's a horrible thing.

I know what's popping into your mind now. What if I go to my neighbor who raises chickens—is it okay to eat those eggs? My answer: Sure. Yeah. *If* your neighbors adopted or rescued those chickens and they're not going to slaughter them once they're not laying eggs, then ethically it's not the same problem. But to tell you the truth, most of the people who raise their own chickens buy them from the same factory farms that are brutally abusive to them. (Sad fact: Did you know that baby chicks are sent to backyard farmers *through the mail*? Yep, they get shipped like objects, subjected to journeys of up to seventy-two hours in a box, with no food or water while exposed to extremes in temperature.) And let's be honest. Most of us are not going to get eggs from our neighbors.

The health factor is also important to consider. One egg, I don't care whether it's labeled "cage-free" or "free-range," has more cholesterol than a double quarter-pounder with cheese. If you eat one egg, you have reached your daily quota of cholesterol. Period. (And by the way, they're gross. They pop out of a female's vagina as part of her menstrual cycle.) Further, people eat eggs because they think they're getting a lot of protein, but one egg only has 6 grams of protein; why not eat a cup of lentils instead, and enjoy 18 grams of protein with some fiber to boot?

Does that mean you should never have an omelet again? That's entirely up to you and what your comfort zone is. You know best what feels right to you. But I promise you, for every egg-based breakfast food you think you'll miss, there's a healthy, delicious vegan pancake or tofu scramble you can enjoy instead.

Isn't eating meat an essential part of human evolution?

We definitely ate meat (but very, very little, as it was hard to come by) as we evolved as human beings. We had to; scarcity of calories was an issue of survival back in the day. Some have said the concentrated calories found in animal foods enabled our brains to develop, but more recent research concludes that it was probably due more to a diet of starchy tubers (edible seeds, leaves and roots, stems, berries, and potato-like things). In any case, we're (hopefully) now smart enough to realize that we aren't starving for calories in the developed world, and it would benefit us to move toward better, cleaner choices—both for our health and the environment. Most important, we've evolved as a culture. We have moved away from appalling injustices like slavery. We've transcended who we were thousands of—and even just a hundred—years ago.

I'm ready to move toward a more veganish diet. What should I give up first?

First, think of it as swapping foods out, rather than "giving things up." It'll be more fun that way! After all, you're eliminating certain foods from your diet in order to make room for a whole new world of delicious veggies, whole grains, and other veganish treats.

Second, although many people tend to stop eating red meat before they give up chicken, turkey, or fish, from a humane standpoint, it should be the other way around. Chickens and turkeys are seriously the most abused animals on the planet, and birds and fish yield less flesh than cows or pigs, so "farmers" and "fishermen" kill more of them to satisfy consumers' meat habits. (I have to put farmers and fishermen in quotes because they really aren't those down-home people we read about in storybooks; nearly everyone in the animal food business these days is connected to a giant corporation, so the quaint, hardworking, honest-folk image no longer fits the industrialized world of Big Food. I actually really respect what farmers and fishermen used to be like, and it's really sad that they've been forced into the industrialized program that exists now. I hope those good people of yesteryear can carve out new lives in a kinder, plant-based world; it would be easier on them, too, as I'm sure it's really hard to keep up with the meaner and more brutal modern systems.) Anyway, if you choose to give up meat in stages, you might want to stop eating chicken and turkey first, then fish, and then pork and beef. Some will suggest that cattle are the worst for the environment, but that seems like hair-splitting to me. Crucial rain forests (like the Amazon) are being cut down to grow soybeans to feed chickens, and the waste from chicken farms is poisoning our environment. When you think about it, it's a lot less efficient to eat chickens who are fed grain than to just eat that grain itself.

However you decide to go, know that there's no "right" order other than making that leap in whatever way feels *right* to you.

A lot of popular vegan foods seem to contain soy. What is it and what do I need to know about eating products with soy in them?

Soy is a bean that comes from a pod (like peas). It's loaded with protein. Women in Okinawa, Japan—one of the populations known to have the longest life spans of anyone on the planet—eat a lot of soy; it is a main staple of their daily diet. Breast cancer is extremely rare there, as is heart disease, and some researchers attribute that to the soy they eat! In China, too, as is the case in much of Asia, soy has been eaten daily for thousands of years, and people fared quite well in terms of avoiding the health problems like diabetes and obesity that plague us in developed parts of the world. (Of course, all that is changing as other countries adopt diets more like our own superprocessed junk-food-laden diet.)

So if you're concerned about eating soy because you've heard you might get man boobs if you're a guy, or breast cancer later in life if you're a gal, don't worry; the overwhelming consensus of science is that soy is not only fine, it's beneficial, especially if it's organic and not too heavily processed. That means it's better to choose tofu over a tofu hot dog, and edamame over soy crisps. If you do prefer to avoid soy, though, you should know that the vast majority of soy grown in the world is fed to animals, so if you consume animals, you're consuming soy anyway. That said, you absolutely don't need soy to be healthy, so feel free to skip it and get your protein from the huge variety of other beans, legumes, and nuts available.

Do I need omega-3 fatty acids from fish or fish oil?

Omega-3s are fatty acids that've been reported to protect your brain and heart. They're found in fish, but also in flax, avocado, soy, walnuts, and algae. To get my omega-3s, I put 2 tablespoons of ground flax in my smoothie every day, and I eat lots of avocado, walnuts, and soy. You could also take a supplement sourced from algae, which is where the fish get their omega-3s! That way, you're not getting all the toxic mercury, saturated fat, and cholesterol that come along with fish *and* you're sparing the fish!

What does "organic" produce mean, technically, and is it okay to eat fruits and vegetables that aren't organic? That stuff's pricey!

"Organic" produce means fruit and vegetables grown without the use of pesticides or synthetic fertilizers. Since my primary concern is compassion for animals, organic is not at the very top of my list; the alleviation of suffering is. But concern for the environment is a close second, and chemicals and pesticides are really bad for the land and water. So I say: If you can afford organic, go for it. But if that label is going to stop you from eating some broccoli, don't let it. Just be sure to thoroughly wash your fresh produce before you eat it. You can also go online to check out which fruits and veggies are the worst—they're called the Dirty Dozen—when not organic, and at least avoid buying them if they're conventionally grown. (Conventionally grown = code for "pesticides used.") By the way, if something is labeled "organic," it also means it's GMO-free. GMO stands for "genetically modified organism."

What happens to jobs in the animal agriculture business if everyone goes vegan? Aren't they crucial to our economy?

Being successful—as an individual or a business—means we constantly have to adapt. Once electricity was discovered, whale oil became obsolete. If you were in the whale oil business and continued to insist it was the best way to light lanterns, you'd be in trouble. Typewriters gave way to laptops and telegraphs gave way to smart phones. You get the drift. What's really exciting now is that we are at a place in time where technology and industry are primed for the next stage of environment- and animal-friendly innovations. There are businesses waiting to be born, and consumers waiting for things to get easier and healthier. The world is going that way.

Some vegan foods make me kind of gassy. What can I do to avoid that?

Hey, you're making big changes to your diet here, so give that body of yours a chance to adjust to all the fabulous new fiber you're introducing into your diet. ("A chance to adjust" = a nicer way of saying "you might be a little gassy for a month or so.") You're detoxing from old ways, and your body is trying to get rid of stuff. It's not always pretty, but it's worth it. Your body *will* adjust, I promise. Soon.

It's true, beans can make you a little gassy if you're not used to them. But beans should *not* be excluded from your diet, because they're great sources of protein, calcium, and iron, among other nutrients. Start off by eating them in small portions, and always very well cooked. (If you're cooking dried beans, be sure to soak them in water for at least several hours first and then toss the soaking water; this will be a big help.) Beans should be very soft, with no hint of crunchiness. Chew well. (Fun fact: Digestion begins in the mouth. As the teeth grind the food, a digestive enzyme called amylase in your saliva starts to break down some of the carbohydrates—starches and sugars—in the food even before it leaves the mouth.)

Cruciferous vegetables like broccoli, cauliflower, Brussels sprouts, kale, and cabbage can also cause indigestion for some people. The answer is to cook them thoroughly and add them to your diet gradually. Later on you can start to add in more raw stuff.

Fruits vary. Some people do very well with raw fruit; others have more difficulty at first. If you are new to any particular fruit, have smaller servings at first, and then gradually increase.

Once you're used to all the fabulous fiber you'll be eating (which keeps you lean, strong, steady, and clean), you won't be gassy. It's just a temporary adjustment. Some people swear by Beano, a digestive enzyme that prevents gas and stomach bloating; you can get it in any drugstore, and it's affordable.

I work out a lot and I've heard that animal protein is fundamental to building strength. Can I eat veganish and still be strong?

Oh, I'm so glad you are wondering about this, because this is one of the most talked about aspects of a plant-centric diet. I want to introduce you to a friend of mine who really explains it well. Meet Robert Cheeke, a kick-ass body builder who credits his vegan diet for his amazing physique!

SHRED IT!

Robert Cheeke is the best-selling author of *Shred It!* and *Vegan Bodybuilding & Fitness*, a two-time champion bodybuilder, and the founder/president of Vegan Bodybuilding & Fitness (www.veganbodybuilding.com).

Isn't that inspiring? You can actually have it all—a great body, delicious food, *and* live your truth!

KF: Tell me how you got from skinny teen to your muscle-bound self!

RC: When I became vegan in 1995, I was 15 years old and weighed 120 pounds. Seven years later I weighed 195 pounds and went on to win multiple bodybuilding competitions. I was able to achieve muscle-building success on a vegan diet because I was consistent with my training and nutrition programs. I understood I needed to consume more calories than I was expending and that they needed to come from high-quality sources. As it turns out, the original sources of nutrition (vitamins, minerals, amino acids, fatty acids, glucose, and other essential nutrients) come in their optimal form in plant-based whole foods (fruits, vegetables, nuts, grains, seeds, and legumes).

KF: Why is being veganish better than eating animal protein?

RC: Plant-based foods are not very calorically dense, but are extremely nutrient-dense. The statistics are pretty straightforward; plant-based foods are lower in

(continued)

calories and higher in nutrition, and animal-based foods are higher in calories and lower in nutritional yield.

KF: **Do you do dairy and eggs? Fish? If not, why not?**

RC: I became vegan twenty years ago because I did not want to contribute to animal suffering. All beings have the ability to experience pain, fear, and suffering, and since age fifteen I have dedicated my life to reducing animal suffering and saving animal lives.

Over the two decades that I have not consumed animal-based foods I have gained seventy-five pounds (mostly muscle) and competed at INBA Natural Bodybuilding World Championships. I have placed in the top five in every running race I have competed in over the past ten years and set a course record in a three-hour timed race in 2012 that still stands today. I found success in both strength and endurance sports fueled exclusively by plants. No animals have to suffer for me to achieve my health and fitness goals, and I work hard to lead by positive example.

KF: **How much protein/calories do you get a day?**

RC: When it comes to protein consumption, I follow a 70/15/15 approach, meaning I consume 70 percent of my calories from carbohydrates, 15 percent from protein, and 15 percent from fat, because I believe this is the most balanced, most practical, and optimal approach for overall health and fitness. Therefore, I don't aim for a specific amount of protein, but the amount of protein consumed in a day will be roughly 15 percent of that day's caloric intake. I don't place any special emphasis on protein consumption because protein is so easy to get adequate amounts of. If anything, I try to avoid eating too much protein to lessen the adverse implications a high-protein diet can have on kidneys, liver, bones, and waistline.

KF: **What does a typical day of eating look like?**

RC: A typical day on my whole-food plant-based diet looks like this:

BREAKFAST

- Water
- A few pieces of whole fruit
- A bowl of oats with berries or other fruit
- A green smoothie made from green leafy vegetables, water, and fruit

SNACK

- A few pieces of whole fruit
- Vegetables and hummus
- Yerba mate drink

LUNCH

- International cuisine such as Thai, Indian, or Mexican
- Small green salad
- Water

SNACK

- A few pieces of whole fruit
- A fruit, nut, and seed bar
- Water

DINNER

- Potatoes, lentils, beans, brown rice, quinoa, or other starchy complex-carbohydrate food
- Green salad
- International cuisine
- Water

SNACK

- A few pieces of whole fruit
- A fruit, nut, and seed bar
- Occasionally something heavy such as potatoes, beans, lentils

KF: **What is the ideal meal if you want to shred?**

RC: If you want to get shredded (burn fat while toning muscle), you will want to eat foods that are low on the calorie scale but high in nutrient density. These foods are leafy green vegetables, fruits, starchy vegetables, beans and other legumes.

An ideal meal would be made up of whole-plant foods, low in protein and fat and high in whole-food complex carbohydrates. A meal to get shredded might look like this:

- A few pieces of whole fruit
- Small green salad

- Bowl of yams or sweet potatoes with beans and lentils
- Water

I have always been an athlete since I was a child and the one thing I regret most was not going vegan earlier. I played soccer and ran cross-country and track all throughout high school and I was a top player, but my diet was terrible at that point in my life. I ran so much that I could eat anything I wanted and stay fit, but I had no idea that if I had been respectful to my body and was conscious of what I was eating, I could have been performing on a national level instead of the state and regional levels. I'm now late into college and am the healthiest I have ever been in my life. I go to the gym five to six days a week and have never felt better about my fitness level. Working out on a plant-based lifestyle is so much more satisfying because you know you worked hard to make your gains; but it's so much easier to do because of how much better your body functions. I was an extremely scrawny kid in high school from all the running, but after starting to work out and eating a healthy and balanced plant-based diet, I've gained eighteen pounds of muscle since graduating high school and keep making gains every year. —Hunter, Orlando, FL

Want a glimpse of the future? Check this out: 1 percent of baby boomers are vegetarian; 4 percent of Gen X'ers are vegetarian; 12 percent of millennials are vegetarian. And then there's YOU and yours, so as you can see, the future is getting brighter and better.

You, my dear friend, are a truth seeker, and I respect you so much for this. You are pushing your boundaries of care and concern, and you're taking responsibility for your own health and well-being, and you're stepping up to fix this sweet, crazy, kinda screwed-up world of ours. Thank you for that. I hope you feel empowered and excited, because you are doing something HUGELY important and meaningful. If we have the chance to meet, I know I'll love you. You're a game changer. Go enjoy your life, and spread the good word. I thank you from the bottom of my heart for being so open and willing to make the shift this planet is hungry for.

1% OF BABY BOOMERS ARE VEGETARIAN

4% OF GEN X'ERS ARE VEGETARIAN

12% OF MILLENNIALS ARE VEGETARIAN

THE FUTURE IS BRIGHT

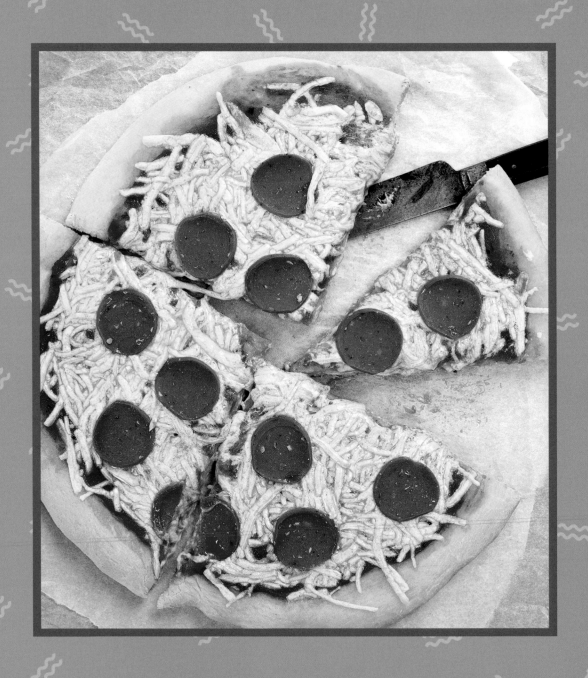

RECIPES

This is where you get to explore some really fantastic food with recipes created by vegan chef and bestselling cookbook author Robin Robertson! She's a genius at coming up with quick, hearty, healthy, delicious, affordable recipes that can feed you and some friends for one meal, or be your lunch or dinner over the course of several days. She comes up with incredible flavor combinations, and man, does she know how to veganize so many of our favorite foods!

Robin designed the recipes in this book using simple, easy-to-find ingredients—you probably already have a lot of them in your kitchen! The recipes are easy, delicious, and pack some serious nutrition. She's got you covered on all bases: Breakfast, Lunch, Dinner, Snacks, Soups, Treats. *Anyone* can make these recipes, even if they have no cooking experience whatsoever. Seasoned cooks will love them, too, because the recipes are simple and have great variety and flavor. Most of all, they're fun—both to make and, more important, to eat!

BREAKFAST

Add a squeeze
of lime juice

SALSA BREAKFAST BURRITOS

What's more satisfying in the morning than a breakfast burrito? This one is loaded with protein and gets some nice flavor punch from the scallions and salsa (and hot sauce, if you like your kick extra hard). The filling makes enough for two burritos, so if you only need one, save the other to heat up in the microwave for a later meal, or tomorrow's breakfast.

MAKES 2 SERVINGS

1 tablespoon extra-virgin olive oil

3 scallions, chopped

14 ounces firm tofu, drained and crumbled

½ teaspoon salt

¼ teaspoon ground black pepper

2 tablespoons nutritional yeast

¾ cup chunky tomato salsa

½ cup shredded vegan cheese, such as Daiya brand (optional)

2 large flour tortillas

Hot sauce, for serving (optional)

Heat the olive oil in a medium skillet over medium-high heat. Add the scallions and cook for 3 minutes to soften. Add the tofu, salt, and pepper. Cook, stirring, to heat through and blend flavors, about 5 minutes. Sprinkle on the nutritional yeast and cook until any liquid has evaporated. Stir in the salsa, then sprinkle on the vegan cheese (if using). Cook for 1 to 2 minutes longer to heat through.

To serve, divide the tofu mixture between the tortillas, spooning the mixture just below the center of each tortilla. Splash on hot sauce, if desired, then carefully fold in the sides over the filling, and roll to enclose.

ROASTED RED PEPPER SCRAMBLE

A tofu scramble is a great protein-boosted meal for breakfast or any time of the day. It's delicious, but also versatile—you can throw in the ingredients listed below, or whatever looks good to you that you've got in your kitchen. Think about it this way: If it's a veggie you'd throw into an egg omelet or scramble, throw it into a tofu scramble!

MAKES 2 TO 3 SERVINGS

1 tablespoon extra-virgin olive oil

2 scallions, chopped

½ cup chopped jarred roasted red pepper

14 ounces firm tofu, drained and crumbled

3 tablespoons nutritional yeast

½ teaspoon salt

¼ teaspoon ground black pepper

⅛ teaspoon ground turmeric

⅛ teaspoon paprika

⅓ cup shredded vegan cheese, such as Daiya brand (optional)

Heat the olive oil in a large skillet over medium heat. Add the scallions and cook until softened, about 3 minutes. Stir in the roasted pepper, crumbled tofu, nutritional yeast, salt, black pepper, turmeric, and paprika. Cook, stirring, until the mixture is dry and the ingredients are hot, about 10 minutes. Stir in the cheese (if using). Taste and add salt and black pepper, if needed. Serve hot.

VARIATIONS: In addition to (or instead of) the roasted red pepper, add any chopped cooked vegetables you have on hand (broccoli and zucchini are good choices), or sauté a handful of baby spinach or sliced mushrooms along with the scallions. Chopped tomato is also a good addition, as are your favorite fresh or dried herbs.

EGGLESS BENEDICT BOWLS

Here's a new and improved take on classic eggs Benedict. This veganized version is super convenient to make, so cozy to eat, and also works great as a brunch dish or late-night supper.

MAKES 2 SERVINGS

⅓ cup vegan mayonnaise

2 tablespoons vegan butter, such as Earth Balance brand, at room temperature

2 teaspoons fresh lemon juice

½ teaspoon Dijon mustard

¼ teaspoon ground turmeric

Salt and ground black pepper

12 ounces firm tofu, drained and patted dry

2 tablespoons nutritional yeast

1 tablespoon all-purpose flour

½ teaspoon smoked paprika

1 tablespoon extra-virgin olive oil, or more if needed

4 slices vegan bacon, cut into 1-inch squares

2 slices whole-grain bread

In a small bowl, combine the mayonnaise, butter, lemon juice, mustard, ⅛ teaspoon of the turmeric, and salt and pepper to taste. Mix well and set the sauce aside.

Cut the tofu into ½-inch cubes. In a bowl, combine the nutritional yeast, flour, paprika, remaining ⅛ teaspoon turmeric, and salt and pepper to taste and mix well. Add the tofu and toss to coat.

Heat the olive oil in a medium skillet over medium-high heat. Add the tofu and cook until golden brown all over, 8 to 10 minutes. Remove from the skillet and set aside.

Return the skillet to the heat and add a little more oil, if needed. Add the bacon and cook until hot and lightly browned on both sides, about 1 minute. Return the tofu to the skillet with the bacon and keep warm.

Heat the reserved sauce in a microwave until warm, about 30 seconds. If you don't have a microwave, heat the sauce in a small saucepan over low heat until warm. (You can also just use it at room temperature.)

Toast the bread and cut it into 1-inch squares. Divide the toast squares between two bowls, then add the tofu and bacon, dividing the mixture evenly. Spoon half the sauce on top of each bowl and serve immediately.

EASY OATMEAL BOWL

Don't tell your mom I said this, but our version of this classic breakfast is yummier than what she made when you were a kid, and offers a lot more variety. It also couldn't be easier to make! Try substituting almond or cashew milk for all or half the water for extra flavor.

MAKES 1 SERVING

½ cup old-fashioned rolled oats or quick-cooking oats (not instant)

Salt

Optional Toppings:

Dried fruit (raisins or cranberries)

Chopped nuts (walnuts, pecans, or almonds)

Fresh fruit (sliced banana or strawberries)

Peanut butter or almond butter

Granola

Fruit-sweetened jam

Pure maple syrup

Plain, unsweetened nondairy milk

Soy or coconut yogurt

Ground cinnamon

Stovetop Method: Combine 1 cup water, the oats, and a pinch of salt in a small saucepan and bring to a boil over medium-high heat. Reduce the heat to low and simmer, stirring, for 5 minutes (if using quick-cooking oats) or 10 minutes (for rolled oats), or until it's as thick as you like it. Transfer to a bowl and add your favorite toppings.

Microwave Method: In a microwave-safe bowl, combine the water, oats, and a pinch of salt. Microwave on High for 2 minutes (for quick-cooking oats) or 3 minutes (for rolled oats). Remove from the microwave and stir. Add your favorite toppings.

CRANBERRY AND ALMOND BUTTER OVERNIGHT OATS

This dish is quick to make, and hits that sweet spot of major delish and nutrient-rich. Make it the night before for a to-go breakfast the next morning. The optional chia or flax seeds help to thicken the oats and add nutrients. Substitute peanut butter if you don't have almond butter, and raisins or other dried or fresh fruit for the dried cranberries.

MAKES 1 SERVING

½ cup old-fashioned rolled oats

½ cup plain or vanilla almond milk or other nondairy milk

⅓ cup dried cranberries

1 tablespoon pure maple syrup

1 teaspoon chia seeds or ground flax seeds (optional)

2 tablespoons almond butter or peanut butter

Optional Toppings:

Vegan yogurt

Sliced banana

In your favorite cereal bowl, combine the oats, almond milk, cranberries, maple syrup, and chia seeds (if using). Stir in the almond butter (no need to mix it in completely; it's okay to leave some streaks of almond butter throughout the oat mixture). Cover the bowl and refrigerate overnight. It will be ready to enjoy the next morning or as soon as 6 hours later or up to 12 hours later. Serve as is or top with yogurt or banana, if desired.

RED BEAN AND SWEET POTATO HASH

Red beans and sweet potatoes is an irresistible combo of fun flavor and serious nutrient goodness—and a great way to use up a leftover sweet potato if you have one hanging out in your fridge. You can also substitute any other kind of potato (raw or baked) to use up what's already in your kitchen—or what your potato-loving taste buds might prefer.

MAKES 4 SERVINGS

1 tablespoon extra-virgin olive oil

1 medium onion, chopped

2 garlic cloves, very finely chopped

1 large sweet potato (8 ounces), cooked (see Chef's Tip), peeled, and diced

½ teaspoon dried thyme

½ teaspoon dried oregano

Salt and ground black pepper

1 (15-ounce) can dark red kidney beans, drained and rinsed

Heat the olive oil in a large skillet over medium-high heat. Add the onion and cook until softened, about 5 minutes. Add the garlic and cook for 1 minute longer, then stir in the sweet potato, thyme, oregano, and salt and pepper to taste.

Place the beans in a bowl and mash them with a fork or potato ricer. Add the mashed beans to the skillet and stir to combine with the onion mixture. Cook, turning frequently, then pressing the spatula down on the mixture, until the bottom is lightly crisped and browned when turned, about 10 minutes. Serve hot.

CHEF'S TIP:

For this recipe, the sweet potato should be tender but still firm enough to dice.

To bake sweet potatoes: Preheat the oven to 400°F. Pierce the sweet potatoes with a fork in three places. Wrap each sweet potato in aluminium foil and bake for 45 minutes to 1 hour (depending on the size of the potatoes) or until tender.

To microwave sweet potatoes: If you don't have a cooked sweet potato (or the 45 minutes to an hour it takes to bake one), you can microwave one in minutes: Pierce the sweet potato with a fork in three places. Place the potato on a microwavable plate and microwave on high for 5 minutes, rotating halfway through. You may need to microwave it a minute or two longer, depending on the size of the potato, until it is tender.

Toast Me!

APPLE-WALNUT BREAKFAST BREAD

Slightly sweet, oil-free, and totally satisfying, this makes a great breakfast on the run. I know you want to eat it all in one sitting (I do, too), so to avoid that calorie splurge, cut it into single servings, wrap in plastic wrap, and put them in the freezer until needed. This also makes a great baked gift. Wrap it up and tie it with a bow—now you're everyone's favorite breakfast baker.

MAKES 8 SERVINGS

1½ cups unsweetened applesauce

¾ cup packed light brown sugar

⅓ cup plain, unsweetened almond milk or other nondairy milk

1 tablespoon ground flax seeds mixed with 2 tablespoons warm water

2 cups all-purpose flour

1 teaspoon baking soda

½ teaspoon baking powder

1 teaspoon salt

1 teaspoon ground cinnamon

¾ cup chopped walnuts

Preheat the oven to 375°F. Lightly oil a 9 x 5-inch loaf pan and set aside.

In a large bowl, combine the applesauce, brown sugar, almond milk, and flax mixture and stir until smooth and well mixed. Set aside.

In a separate bowl, combine the flour, baking soda, baking powder, salt, and cinnamon. Mix the dry ingredients into the wet ingredients just until blended. Stir in the walnuts, then transfer the batter to the prepared pan, spreading it evenly and smoothing the top.

Bake until golden brown and a toothpick inserted into the center comes out clean, 25 to 30 minutes. Cool in the pan for about 20 minutes, then remove from the pan and cool completely on a wire rack.

PEANUT BUTTER AND BANANA SMOOTHIE

There might not be any food combination more satisfyingly healthy and energy producing than peanut butter and banana. Throw those two into a blender, and you're in smoothie heaven.

MAKES 1 SERVING

1 ripe banana, cut into chunks and frozen

½ cup frozen kale or spinach leaves

1 tablespoon chocolate protein powder (optional)

1 tablespoon peanut butter

1 cup plain, unsweetened nondairy milk

½ cup nondairy vanilla yogurt (or ½ cup more nondairy milk)

Combine all the ingredients in a blender and blend until smooth. Pour into a large glass and serve.

CHEF'S TIP:

Secret smoothie trick: Use frozen fruits and vegetables to make it cold and thick without the need for ice. Plan ahead and measure out bananas, kale, or other fruits and veggies and freeze them in individual freezer bags so you can be ready to satisfy any smoothie emergency quickly (and use up produce that might have gone to waste otherwise!). For extra nutritional value, throw in some vegan protein powder (I like Sun Warrior brand). If you don't have protein powder, add a tablespoon of your favorite nut butter for that extra flavor and protein boost.

VARIATIONS: Use different frozen fruit instead of, or in addition to, the banana, such as blueberries, strawberries, and mango. Use a different nut butter such as almond butter instead of peanut butter.

SOUPS, STEWS, AND CHILI

MINESTRONE IN MINUTES

Ridiculously easy? Check. Also incredibly flavorful and satisfying? Check.

This is a delicious, make-it-your-own Italian vegetable soup. Add vegetables or beans you want to use up, or a small amount of cooked rice or pasta—just place it in the bottom of your bowl and ladle the hot soup on top. To save time, you can even use frozen mixed vegetables to replace the carrots, celery, and zucchini. This soup reheats well, so enjoy it throughout the week.

MAKES 4 SERVINGS

1 tablespoon extra-virgin olive oil

1 large onion, chopped

2 medium carrots, chopped

1 celery stalk, chopped

2 large garlic cloves, minced

1 (14.5-ounce) can diced tomatoes, undrained

1 (15.5-ounce) can cannellini beans (or other white beans), drained and rinsed

1 medium zucchini, diced

4 cups vegetable broth

1 teaspoon dried basil

½ teaspoon dried oregano

Salt and ground black pepper

Heat the olive oil in a large saucepan over medium heat. Add the onion, carrots, celery, and garlic and cook, stirring occasionally, until softened, about 7 minutes. Stir in the tomatoes and their juices, beans, zucchini, and broth. Add the basil, oregano, and salt and pepper to taste. Bring to a boil, then reduce the heat to low and simmer until the vegetables are tender, about 20 minutes. Taste and adjust the seasonings, adding more salt and pepper if needed. Serve hot.

LOADED POTATO SOUP

This soup is a total sneak. It has a really satisfying taste like baked potatoes, but even when loaded with indulgent toppings (if you so choose), it's still low in fat; and because it's vegan, it has no cholesterol.

MAKES 4 SERVINGS

1 pound baking potatoes (2 or 3 large)

1 tablespoon extra-virgin olive oil

4 slices vegan bacon (such as LightLife Smart Bacon), chopped, or ½ cup vegan bacon bits (see Note)

3 cups plain, unsweetened almond or soy milk

½ teaspoon onion powder

½ teaspoon garlic powder

½ teaspoon smoked paprika (optional)

Salt and ground black pepper

2 tablespoons minced scallions

¾ cup vegan sour cream and/or shredded vegan cheddar cheese, such as Daiya brand (optional)

Preheat the oven to 400°F. Place the potatoes in the oven and bake until soft, 45 to 60 minutes. Remove the baked potatoes and set aside to cool slightly.

(If using bacon bits, you can skip this next step.) While the potatoes are baking, heat the olive oil in a skillet over medium heat. Add the vegan bacon and cook until lightly crisped. Do not overcook. Remove the bacon from the skillet and set aside.

Heat the milk in a large saucepan over medium heat.

Halve the baked potatoes lengthwise. Use a spoon to scoop out the insides of the potatoes and add them to the hot milk along with the onion powder, garlic powder, and smoked paprika (if using). Use a potato masher or wooden spoon to mash the potatoes in the pot, leaving them somewhat chunky. Season with salt and pepper to taste.

Simmer over medium heat until thickened, stirring frequently to keep it from scorching or burning, about 10 minutes. Stir in half the bacon. Ladle the hot soup into bowls and sprinkle with the remaining bacon, the scallions, and, if desired, the sour cream and/or vegan cheddar.

Note: If using bacon bits such as Bac~Os, you can eliminate the olive oil and the sauté step—the bacon bits can be added to the soup "as is."

TORTILLA CHIP SOUP

Say *hola* to this flavorful soup. To save time, omit the seitan and just add an extra can of beans.

MAKES 4 SERVINGS

2 tablespoons extra-virgin olive oil

1 small onion, chopped

3 garlic cloves, minced

1 jalapeño, seeded and minced

1 (14.5-ounce) can fire-roasted diced tomatoes, undrained

1 (15-ounce) can black beans, drained and rinsed

4 cups vegetable broth

Salt and ground black pepper

8 ounces seitan or vegan "chicken" strips (such as Gardein brand), cut into bite-size pieces

Juice of 2 limes

½ cup chopped fresh cilantro

2 cups broken tortilla or corn chips

1 Hass avocado, pitted, peeled, and diced

Heat 1 tablespoon of the olive oil in a pot over medium heat. Add the onion and cook until soft, about 5 minutes. Stir in the garlic and jalapeño and cook for 1 minute. Stir in the tomatoes and their juices, the beans, and the broth and bring to a boil. Reduce the heat to maintain a simmer and cook for 15 minutes. Season with salt and pepper to taste.

While the soup is simmering, heat the remaining 1 tablespoon oil in a skillet over medium heat. Add the seitan and cook until browned, about 4 minutes per side. Set aside.

When you are ready to serve the soup, stir in the lime juice, cilantro, and seitan. Taste and add more salt and pepper if needed. Ladle the soup into bowls and top with the broken tortilla chips and avocado.

GAZPACHO PLUS

Gazpacho is a tomato lover's warm-weather soup dream. The "plus" comes from the extra boost of protein of cooked chickpeas. Throw it together ahead of time, then refrigerate to chill and meld the flavors. Serve it smooth or chunky, and add Tabasco sauce if you like some extra kick.

MAKES 4 TO 6 SERVINGS

2 pounds tomatoes, cored and coarsely chopped (reserve ½ cup chopped tomato for garnish)

1 red bell pepper, coarsely chopped

½ English cucumber, peeled, seeded, and coarsely chopped (reserve ½ cup chopped cucumber for garnish)

2 garlic cloves, minced

3 scallions, chopped

½ jalapeño, seeded and coarsely chopped (optional)

1 tablespoon chopped capers

2 tablespoons sherry vinegar

1 tablespoon extra-virgin olive oil

Salt and ground black pepper

1 (15.5-ounce) can chickpeas, drained and rinsed

1 teaspoon Tabasco sauce (optional)

In a large bowl, combine the tomatoes, bell pepper, cucumber, garlic, scallions, and jalapeño (if using). Add the capers, vinegar, olive oil, and salt and black pepper to taste. Stir to combine. Cover and refrigerate for 3 hours or until chilled. Serve as is or puree in a blender until smooth. To serve, place ⅓ to ½ cup of the chickpeas in a bowl, ladle gazpacho over the chickpeas, and garnish with a spoonful of the reserved chopped tomato and cucumber. Splash on some Tabasco, if desired.

Chili today, lunch tamale

BBQ BLACK BEAN CHILI

What?! A vat of hearty, tasty chili using only five ingredients that can be ready to eat in less time than it takes to order takeout? You better believe it! And it tastes even better reheated; or freeze the extra stash for later.

Serve up this chili with crackers or vegan cornbread, or over cooked pasta or grains (like rice or quinoa). Look for textured vegetable protein (TVP) in the bulk section of well-stocked supermarkets or natural foods stores. It's cheap, easy to store, loaded with protein, and has that salivation-inducing look and texture of ground beef in chili.

MAKES 4 TO 6 SERVINGS

1 cup textured vegetable protein (TVP)

1 (24-ounce) jar chunky tomato salsa (mild, medium, or hot)

2 (15.5-ounce) cans black beans, drained and rinsed

2 tablespoons chili powder

½ cup barbecue sauce, or more if needed

In a heatproof bowl, combine the TVP with enough boiling water to cover and set aside for 10 minutes to rehydrate. Drain.

In a pot, combine the salsa, black beans, chili powder, and barbecue sauce. Stir in the rehydrated TVP and mix well. Cover and cook over medium heat, stirring occasionally, for 15 to 20 minutes, to heat through and blend the flavors. Taste and adjust the seasonings, if needed, adding a little more barbecue sauce if desired. Serve hot.

VARIATIONS: Instead of the TVP, add 8 ounces sautéed crumbled tempeh or chopped cooked butternut squash or sweet potato.

HEARTY PEANUT AND RED BEAN STEW

Peanut butter is the superstar of this supersatisfying stew made with kidney beans, sweet potatoes, and kale. The optional cayenne adds some heat, but leave it out if you prefer to go mild.

MAKES 4 SERVINGS

4 cups chopped kale or spinach

1 tablespoon extra-virgin olive oil

1 large yellow onion, chopped

1 large sweet potato, peeled and cut into ½-inch chunks

1 large red bell pepper, chopped

2 garlic cloves, minced

1 teaspoon grated fresh ginger

½ teaspoon ground cumin

¼ teaspoon cayenne pepper (optional)

1 (14.5-ounce) can fire-roasted diced tomatoes, undrained

2 cups vegetable broth

Salt

1 (15.5-ounce) can dark red kidney beans, drained and rinsed

⅓ cup peanut butter

¼ cup chopped roasted peanuts

Steam the kale in a steamer basket over boiling water until tender, about 5 minutes. Drain well, pressing out any remaining liquid, and set aside.

Heat the olive oil in a large pot over medium heat. Add the onion and cook until softened, about 5 minutes. Add the sweet potato, bell pepper, and garlic. Cover and cook until softened, about 5 minutes. Stir in the ginger, cumin, and cayenne (if using), and cook for 30 seconds. Stir in the tomatoes and their juices, the broth, and salt to taste. Bring to a boil, then reduce the heat to low, add the kidney beans, and simmer until the vegetables are soft, about 30 minutes.

In a small bowl, thin out the peanut butter with 1 cup of the hot liquid from the stew, stirring until blended, then stir the mixture back into the pot. Add the cooked kale, stirring to incorporate. Serve hot, sprinkled with the roasted peanuts.

Eat your kale!

CREAMY TOMATO SOUP

Remember that canned tomato soup you used to have as a kid? This one is way better! In addition to tasting great and being easy and quick to make, it gets a flavorful protein boost from the addition of white beans.

MAKES 4 SERVINGS

1 tablespoon extra-virgin olive oil

1 small onion, chopped

2 garlic cloves, chopped

1 (28-ounce) can crushed tomatoes

1 (15-ounce) can cannellini beans, drained and rinsed

1 teaspoon dried basil

1½ cups vegetable broth

Salt and ground black pepper

Heat the olive oil in a large saucepan over medium heat. Add the onion and cook, stirring often, until softened, about 5 minutes. Add the garlic and cook until fragrant, about 1 minute. Add the tomatoes, beans, basil, and broth. Increase the heat to high and bring to a boil, then reduce the heat to maintain a simmer and cook for 10 minutes. Season with salt and pepper to taste.

Working in batches, carefully transfer the soup to a blender and puree until smooth (or use an immersion blender to puree it right in the pot). Return the pureed soup to the saucepan and cook over low heat until hot, about 5 minutes. Serve hot.

SALADS

shake
shake
shake!

MARINATED BEAN SALAD TO GO

You want a delish lunch salad but no wilty lettuce leaves? Here you go. By layering the salad ingredients with the beans (and any other veggies you want to throw in) on the bottom, the lettuce stays high and dry till you're ready to chomp down.

MAKES 1 SERVING

Dressing:

1 teaspoon minced scallion

½ teaspoon Dijon mustard

½ teaspoon agave nectar

¼ teaspoon dried basil

¼ teaspoon salt

⅛ teaspoon ground black pepper

1½ tablespoons rice vinegar

3 tablespoons extra-virgin olive oil

Salad:

1 (15-ounce) can cannellini beans, drained and rinsed

1 plum tomato, chopped

¼ cup shredded carrot

¼ cup frozen green peas, thawed

2 tablespoons sliced pitted Kalamata olives

2 cups chopped romaine lettuce

In a 3- to 4-cup container with a tight-fitting lid, combine the dressing ingredients, stirring to blend well. Spread the beans on top of the dressing, followed by the tomato, carrot, peas, olives, and lettuce. Place the lid tightly on the container and refrigerate until needed. When ready to serve, shake the salad to distribute the dressing.

¡Olé!

TACO SALAD

Taco + salad?!? Where have you been all my life? This crunchy salad trip is quick and easy to make, and bonus, it's also delicious wrapped in a tortilla or served over rice.

MAKES 2 SERVINGS

½ cup frozen corn kernels, thawed

1 (15.5-ounce) can black beans, drained and rinsed

1 teaspoon taco seasoning

1 scallion, finely minced

¾ cup of your favorite salsa

2 cups finely chopped romaine or iceberg lettuce

1 plum tomato, chopped

1 Hass avocado, pitted, peeled, and diced, or ½ cup guacamole

Salt and ground black pepper

2 tablespoons chopped fresh cilantro (optional)

10 tortilla or corn chips

Lime wedges, for serving

Place the thawed corn in a small bowl with enough boiling water to cover. Let sit for 5 minutes, then drain and set aside.

In a bowl, combine the black beans, taco seasoning, scallion, and ¼ cup of the salsa. Mix well and set aside.

Divide the lettuce between two shallow bowls. Top each with half of the black bean mixture. Spoon half of the chopped tomato, corn, and avocado onto each salad. Divide the remaining salsa between the bowls. Season with salt and pepper and sprinkle on the cilantro (if using). Crumble a handful of the tortilla chips and sprinkle them on top. Serve with lime wedges and more tortilla chips.

Fall for quinoa

AUTUMN QUINOA SALAD

This hearty quinoa salad is chock-full of cozy fall flavors. To save time, cook the quinoa in advance.

MAKES 4 SERVINGS

1½ cups quinoa

Salt and ground black pepper

2 scallions, minced

1 carrot, shredded

1 cup frozen green peas, thawed

1 (15.5-ounce) can dark red kidney beans, drained and rinsed

½ cup unsalted roasted peanuts

½ cup dried cranberries

2 tablespoons extra-virgin olive oil

1 tablespoon rice vinegar

2 tablespoons finely chopped fresh parsley

Bring 3 cups of water to a boil in a saucepan. Add the quinoa and salt to taste. Reduce the heat to maintain a simmer, cover, and cook until the water has been absorbed, about 12 minutes. Remove from the heat and transfer to a large bowl. Stir in the scallions, carrot, and peas, and set aside to come to room temperature.

Add the beans, peanuts, cranberries, olive oil, vinegar, and parsley. Season to taste with salt and pepper and toss to combine.

> VARIATIONS: Substitute cooked brown rice for the quinoa, or a different type of nut in place of the peanuts.

TABBOULEH SALAD

This delicious Middle Eastern favorite couldn't be easier to make. Because bulgur cooks up in just minutes, this hearty salad is easy to put together quickly, making it an excellent on-the-go lunch. Simply pop it into your lunch bag, or devour it as a dinner side.

MAKES 4 SERVINGS

1 cup bulgur

Salt and ground black pepper

2 tomatoes, chopped

1 (15.5-ounce) can chickpeas, drained and rinsed

3 tablespoons chopped fresh parsley

3 tablespoons extra-virgin olive oil

1½ tablespoons fresh lemon juice

Bring 2 cups of water to a boil in a saucepan. Add the bulgur and salt to taste. Reduce the heat to low, cover, and simmer until the water has been absorbed, about 15 minutes. Drain off any remaining water and blot the bulgur with a wadded paper towel to remove excess moisture. Transfer the bulgur to a large bowl and set aside to cool.

Add the tomatoes, chickpeas, and parsley. Drizzle on the olive oil and lemon juice, and season with salt and pepper to taste. Toss well to combine. Serve chilled or at room temperature.

ANTIPASTO SALAD

This hearty meal is loaded with flavor bursts hitting you from all sides. To bulk it up to feed a crowd (or if you want to make lunch for a week), cook 8 ounces of your favorite bite-size pasta shape. Drain and rinse with cold water, drain again, then toss the pasta with the salad.

MAKES 4 SERVINGS

3 tablespoons extra-virgin olive oil

1½ tablespoons fresh lemon juice

½ teaspoon dried basil

¼ teaspoon sugar

Salt and ground black pepper

1 (15.5-ounce) can chickpeas, drained and rinsed

1 garlic clove, minced

1 (6-ounce) jar marinated artichoke hearts, drained

¼ cup pitted Kalamata olives

1 jarred roasted red pepper, cut into strips

4 cups chopped romaine lettuce

1 tomato, diced

½ English cucumber, peeled and thinly sliced

Handful of fresh basil leaves (optional)

In a small bowl, combine the olive oil, lemon juice, basil, sugar, and salt and black pepper to taste. Blend the dressing well.

In a large bowl, combine the chickpeas, garlic, artichokes, olives, and roasted red pepper. Add the lettuce, tomato, cucumber, and basil (if using). Drizzle on the dressing and toss to combine.

RAMEN SLAW WITH TOFU

I don't know about you, but I consider ramen a primary cheap-eats food group, and this take on it has major protein and flavor punch.

Keep some ramen noodles on hand for quick and easy salads like this one. Thanks to bagged slaw mix and baked marinated tofu (both found in most supermarkets), it only takes minutes to assemble.

MAKES 2 TO 4 SERVINGS

1 (3-ounce) package ramen noodles, broken up into 1-inch pieces (seasoning packet discarded)

⅓ cup peanut butter

1 garlic clove, minced

1 teaspoon grated fresh ginger

3 tablespoons rice vinegar

1 tablespoon tamari soy sauce

½ teaspoon sugar

1 (8-ounce) bag cabbage slaw

8 ounces baked marinated tofu, diced

¼ cup slivered almonds, toasted

Place the noodles in a small saucepan of boiling water. Reduce the heat to low and cook until just tender, about 2 minutes. Drain and rinse with cold water, then drain again. Set aside.

In a large bowl, combine the peanut butter, garlic, ginger, vinegar, tamari, sugar, and ⅓ cup water. Whisk the dressing until smooth and well blended.

Add the cooked noodles, slaw, tofu, and almonds to the dressing and toss well to combine.

VARIATIONS: Change it up if you want: Substitute chickpeas for the tofu, leftover cooked pasta for the ramen, or your favorite salad dressing in place of this one.

Rrrrrramen!

pho sure!

BANH MI SALAD BOWLS

This is like going to Vietnam, but cheaper and faster. Savor the bowl version, or for a more filling meal, serve it over toasted French bread or sandwich it in sliced baguette or flatbread. Look for baked marinated tofu in most supermarkets and natural foods stores.

MAKES 2 SERVINGS

2 tablespoons vegan mayonnaise

1 tablespoon hoisin sauce

1 tablespoon rice vinegar

1 teaspoon Sriracha

1 teaspoon fresh lime juice

3 cups shredded cabbage

1 carrot, shredded

8 ounces baked marinated tofu, cut into thin strips

½ cup sliced cucumber

⅓ cup fresh cilantro leaves

2 scallions, minced

1 tablespoon minced jalapeño

In a large bowl, combine the mayo, hoisin, vinegar, Sriracha, and lime juice. Mix well until thoroughly blended. Add the remaining ingredients and toss to combine.

SANDWICHES, WRAPS, AND BURGERS

BETTER BEAN BURGERS

I *know* you didn't think going veganish meant sacrificing great burgers! These bean burgers are loaded with nutrients, and so quick and easy to make. Serve them on burger rolls with your favorite condiments such as ketchup, relish, Vegenaise, and/or pile it high with your fave toppings like Daiya cheese, lettuce, spinach, kale, tomatoes, cucumbers, and shredded carrots!

Save yourself time later and make a double batch of burgers and freeze the extras for future meals!

1 (15-ounce) can pinto, kidney, or black beans, drained, rinsed, and blotted dry with paper towels

½ cup walnut pieces

½ cup quick-cooking oats (not instant)

¼ cup chopped onion

2 tablespoons chopped fresh parsley

2 teaspoons cornstarch

½ teaspoon garlic powder

½ teaspoon ground cumin (optional)

Salt and ground black pepper

1 tablespoon extra-virgin olive oil

Burger rolls, as needed

Optional Toppings:

Lettuce

Sliced tomato

Grilled onion

Sliced Hass avocado

Pickle slices

Ketchup

Mustard

Relish

Sliced vegan cheese

Sautéed vegan bacon

In a food processor, combine the beans, walnuts, oats, onion, parsley, cornstarch, garlic powder, cumin (if using), and salt and pepper to taste. Pulse until well combined but not completely pureed. You want to leave some texture. Pinch a bit of the mixture to make sure it holds together. Divide the mixture into four equal portions and use your hands to shape them into patties. Refrigerate for 20 minutes or longer to firm up.

Heat the olive oil in a large skillet over medium heat. Cook the burgers until browned on both sides, about 5 minutes per side.

LEFTOVERS:

If you're only cooking one burger, wrap the extras individually in plastic wrap and freeze for up to 3 months.

CHICKPEA CAESAR WRAPS

Hail, Caesar! This salad is named for the popular Caesar salad, which contains romaine lettuce and a garlicky lemony dressing. Like the salad version, these wraps are creamy, crunchy, and delicious.

MAKES 2 WRAPS

1 (15.5-ounce) can chickpeas, drained and rinsed

2 garlic cloves, crushed

3 tablespoons fresh lemon juice

1 tablespoon nutritional yeast

1½ teaspoons Dijon mustard

½ teaspoon dried oregano

Salt and ground black pepper

2 large flour tortillas

2 cups shredded romaine lettuce

1 tomato, thinly sliced

1 carrot, shredded

1 Hass avocado, pitted, peeled, and sliced

In a food processor, combine the chickpeas, garlic, lemon juice, nutritional yeast, and mustard, and process until smooth and well combined. Add the oregano and salt and pepper to taste and process to incorporate.

To assemble, divide the chickpea mixture between the tortillas and spread it evenly. Top each with half the lettuce, tomato, carrot, and avocado. Fold the sides in over the filling, then roll to enclose, burrito-style, and slice the wraps in half on an angle. Serve immediately.

LEFTOVERS:

If you're only making one wrap, make the chickpea spread, use half, then cover and refrigerate the rest, but wait to cut the fresh veggies for the second wrap until needed.

CURRIED TOFU SANDWICHES

Make everyone jealous at lunchtime, but give yourself a head start after dinner the night before. This sandwich filling tastes best if made in advance so the flavors have time to develop. I like to keep cashews and raisins on hand for snacking or to toss into salads, so throw some into this if you got 'em (no prob if you don't). If you only want to buy a small amount of nuts or dried fruits, check out the bulk bins at well-stocked supermarkets and natural foods stores.

MAKES 2 SANDWICHES

8 ounces extra-firm tofu, drained and diced

1¼ teaspoons curry powder

¼ teaspoon salt

3 tablespoons vegan mayonnaise

¼ cup shredded carrot

¼ cup minced celery

1 scallion, minced

2 tablespoons chopped roasted cashews

2 tablespoons raisins

4 slices whole-grain bread or 2 pita breads

Lettuce leaves (optional)

Heat 2 tablespoons of water in a skillet over medium heat. Add the tofu and sprinkle with 1 teaspoon of the curry powder and the salt. Cook until the water has evaporated, stirring to coat the tofu with the seasoning. Remove from the heat and set aside to cool.

In a bowl, combine the mayo and remaining ¼ teaspoon curry powder, stirring to blend. Add the carrot, celery, scallion, cashews, raisins, and tofu. Stir to combine thoroughly. Taste and adjust the seasonings if needed.

Spread the mixture onto bread or stuff into pita halves. Add lettuce to the sandwiches, if you like.

LEFTOVERS:
Any extra filling will keep for up to 3 days in the refrigerator in a tightly covered container.

No eggs here

NO-TUNA SALAD SANDWICHES

A standard lunch favorite, made better and healthier. For the best flavor, cover and refrigerate the sandwich filling for at least 30 minutes or overnight to allow the flavors to meld.

MAKES 2 SANDWICHES

1 (14-ounce) jar or can hearts of palm (see Note), drained

⅓ cup chopped celery

2 tablespoons minced red onion

⅓ cup vegan mayonnaise

1 teaspoon Dijon mustard

2 teaspoons fresh lemon juice

Salt and ground black pepper

4 slices sandwich bread

Lettuce and tomato slices

Pulse the hearts of palm in a food processor until finely chopped. Transfer to a bowl and add the celery, onion, mayo, mustard, and lemon juice. Season to taste with salt and pepper, then mix well to combine. Taste and adjust the seasonings if needed. Add a little more mayo if the mixture is too dry.

Pile the filling onto sandwich bread and top with lettuce and tomato slices.

Note: Hearts of palm (the inner portion of the shoot of a type of palm tree) are similar in flavor to artichoke hearts and are available in most supermarkets.

LEFTOVERS:
Any extra filling can be covered and refrigerated for up to 3 days.

PEANUT BUTTER AND MORE SANDWICH

The king of all sandwiches, bedazzled with good-for-you yumminess. The next time you're in the mood for a classic PB&J, think outside the jar with one (or more) of these tasty additions.

MAKES 1 SANDWICH

2 slices whole-grain bread

⅓ cup creamy peanut butter

Choice of Add-ins:

Fruit-sweetened jam (any flavor)

Sliced banana, apple, pear, or peach

Shredded carrot

Minced celery

Thinly sliced cucumber

Cooked vegan bacon

Mango chutney

Roasted sunflower seeds

Raisins or dried cranberries

Grated chocolate

Crushed nuts

Ground flax seeds

Spread each slice of bread with a little peanut butter. Sprinkle with one or more of the add-ins. Top with the second slice, cut the sandwich, and enjoy!

SLOPPY VEGANS

Here's a comfort food favorite, veganized. No time to cook your own lentils? Use canned or precooked lentils (you can find them in the refrigerated section at Trader Joe's if you have one in your area).

MAKES 4 SANDWICHES

1 tablespoon extra-virgin olive oil

1 medium onion, chopped

1 small red or green bell pepper, chopped

2 garlic cloves, minced

2 cups cooked lentils

½ cup ketchup

¼ cup barbecue sauce

1 tablespoon Dijon mustard

1 tablespoon soy sauce

1 tablespoon red wine vinegar

2 teaspoons light brown sugar

1 teaspoon chili powder

Salt and ground black pepper

4 sandwich rolls, split

Heat the olive oil in a large skillet over medium heat. Add the onion and cook until softened, about 5 minutes. Stir in the bell pepper and garlic and cook for 3 to 4 minutes longer to soften the vegetables.

Stir in the lentils, ketchup, barbecue sauce, mustard, soy sauce, and vinegar. Add the brown sugar, chili powder, and salt and black pepper to taste. Simmer for 10 minutes, stirring frequently. Taste and adjust the seasonings, if needed. Add a little water if the mixture gets too thick. To serve, spoon the lentil mixture onto sandwich rolls.

VARIATION: You can swap out the lentils for fresh or frozen vegan burger crumbles.

LEFTOVERS:
Leftover sandwich filling can be stored in a tightly sealed container in the refrigerator for 3 to 4 days or in the freezer for 3 months.

Loads o' lentils

Midnight snack star

SPINACH AND WHITE BEAN QUESADILLA

I bet you didn't think a quesadilla made without cheese could be so healthy, nutrient-packed, *and* delicious. This recipe will make the case that it *can*, in all the most satisfying ways.

MAKES 2 QUESADILLAS

1 (15.5-ounce) can cannellini or great northern beans, drained and rinsed

1 tablespoon extra-virgin olive oil

2 garlic cloves, minced

4 cups fresh spinach leaves

Salt and ground black pepper

2 flour tortillas

Place the beans in a large bowl and mash with a wooden spoon or potato masher.

Heat the olive oil in a skillet over medium heat. Add the garlic and cook until fragrant, about 30 seconds. Add the spinach and cook, stirring, until wilted. Add the beans to the spinach mixture. Season with salt and pepper and stir to combine and heat through. Transfer the filling mixture back to the bowl in which you mashed the beans. Rinse out the skillet and return it to the heat.

Spread half of the spinach mixture on a tortilla and fold it in half to enclose the filling. Place the quesadilla in the hot skillet and cook until lightly browned on both sides, turning once. Transfer to a plate and serve hot. Repeat with the remaining filling and tortilla.

STUFFED PORTOBELLO BURGERS

Portobellos stuffed with a flavorful burger filling makes a unique, hearty sandwich. Or try this as a main dish topped with grilled onion and Mushroom Gravy (page 215).

MAKES 2 BURGERS

2 large portobello mushrooms, stems removed

1 tablespoon extra-virgin olive oil, plus more for brushing mushrooms

2 garlic cloves, minced

2 scallions, chopped

¼ cup walnut pieces

1 cup cooked lentils or black beans, blotted dry with paper towels

3 tablespoons dried breadcrumbs

1 tablespoon minced fresh parsley

1 tablespoon nutritional yeast

Salt and ground black pepper

2 burger rolls

Lettuce leaves, sliced tomato, grilled onion, ketchup, mustard

Preheat the oven to 375°F. Line a baking sheet with parchment paper.

Place the mushroom caps on the baking sheet, underside down. Brush the mushrooms lightly with olive oil and bake for 10 minutes to soften. Remove from the oven, but leave the oven on.

While the mushrooms are baking, heat the olive oil in a small skillet over medium heat. Add the garlic and scallions and cook for 3 minutes to soften. Remove from the heat.

Grind the walnuts in a blender or food processor or place them in a plastic sandwich bag and crush them with a rolling pin or the side of a heavy bottle. Transfer the ground walnuts to a bowl. Add the lentils or beans and mash them to break them up. Add the sautéed garlic mixture, breadcrumbs, parsley, nutritional yeast, and salt and pepper to taste. Mix well, then divide the mixture in half and press into balls.

When the mushrooms come out of the oven, flip them over and leave them on the baking sheet. Flatten each of the stuffing balls with your hands, then stuff the mushrooms with the mixture, pressing gently to fit in all the stuffing and smoothing the tops. Return the mushrooms to the oven and bake for 15 minutes.

Serve hot on burger rolls, with your choice of condiments.

LEFTOVERS:

If you want to save one of the burgers for another meal, cook it completely and cool to room temperature, then wrap and freeze.

DINNER SPECIALS

Want!

TACO TIME

It's never not a great time for tacos, right?

1 tablespoon extra-virgin olive oil

1 small onion, chopped

3 garlic cloves, minced

8 ounces tempeh (or other vegan protein; see Note), finely chopped

1 cup chopped mushrooms

1 tablespoon chili powder or taco seasoning

1 teaspoon ground cumin (if using chili powder)

½ teaspoon dried oregano

½ teaspoon salt

6 corn tortillas

Tomato salsa

Shredded lettuce

Guacamole or 1 Hass avocado, pitted, peeled, and diced

Heat the olive oil in a skillet over medium heat. Add the onion and cook until softened, about 5 minutes. Add the garlic and cook for 1 minute longer, then stir in the tempeh and cook for 5 minutes, stirring often. Add the mushrooms, then sprinkle on the chili powder or taco seasoning, cumin (if using chili powder), oregano, and salt. Stir in ½ cup of water and cook for a few minutes longer, until the mixture is nearly dry. Remove from the heat.

One at a time, place the tortillas on top of the tempeh mixture to warm. Fill the tortillas with the tempeh mixture and top with salsa, lettuce, and guacamole to taste.

Note: Instead of tempeh, you can substitute reconstituted TVP, refrigerated or frozen burger crumbles, chopped seitan, or refried beans.

NACHOS FOR DINNER

Yes, you read that right. NACHOS FOR DINNER! And a fun way to use up leftover chili or refried beans. This recipe is more of a guideline—make as much as you need just for you or for a crowd. It will be immediately devoured. Note that you need to soak the cashews for the cream for at least four hours.

MAKES 2 TO 4 SERVINGS

Cheesy Nacho Sauce:

1 cup soaked cashews

2 tablespoons coconut oil

1 small onion, chopped

2 garlic cloves, minced

1 chipotle chile in adobo sauce, chopped

1 teaspoon paprika

½ teaspoon ground cumin

½ teaspoon salt, plus more as needed

1 cup plain, unsweetened almond milk, or more as needed

3 tablespoons nutritional yeast

2 teaspoons fresh lemon juice

Place the cashews in a small bowl and add enough water to cover them. Soak for 4 hours, then drain.

Make the nacho sauce:

Heat the coconut oil in a skillet over medium heat. Add the onion and cook until beginning to soften, about 5 minutes. Add the garlic and cook until the onion and garlic are soft, 1 to 2 minutes. Stir in the chipotle chile, paprika, cumin, and salt, then remove from the heat.

In a blender or food processor, combine the cashews and almond milk and puree until very smooth. Add the sautéed onion mixture, nutritional yeast, and lemon juice and process until completely smooth. If necessary, add more almond milk 1 tablespoon at a time to reach the desired consistency. Taste and add more salt, if needed.

Assembly:

Tortilla chips

Vegan chili (your favorite), refried beans, or cooked pinto or black beans

Toppings: Tomato salsa, guacamole, sliced pitted black olives, chopped tomatoes, chopped scallions or red onion, sliced pickled jalapeño, chopped fresh cilantro

Assemble the dish:

Preheat the oven to 375°F. Spread a layer of tortilla chips in a pie plate or shallow baking dish.

Top the chips with a layer of chili or beans. Spoon all of the nacho sauce on top and bake for 15 minutes to heat through.

Remove from the oven and layer on your choice of toppings.

Waste not, want not

USE-IT-UP FRIED RICE

Clean out your fridge with this recipe. Fried rice is best made with cold rice, so this is a fantastic way to use up leftover cooked rice. It's also an easy solution for using up that half block of tofu that's hanging out in the fridge, along with any leftover veggies you might have.

MAKES 2 SERVINGS

1 tablespoon neutral-tasting vegetable oil

1 medium onion, chopped

4 to 6 ounces extra-firm tofu (about ½ block), drained and crumbled

2 tablespoons soy sauce

2 cups cold cooked rice

1 cup cooked broccoli or other vegetable (optional)

½ cup frozen green peas, thawed

Salt and ground black pepper

1 teaspoon dark sesame oil

Heat the oil in a large skillet or wok over medium-high heat. When it's very hot, add the onion and stir-fry until tender, about 5 minutes.

Stir in the tofu, soy sauce, and rice and mix well. Add the cooked veggies (if using) and the peas. Season with salt and pepper to taste, then drizzle with the sesame oil and cook, stirring, for 5 minutes to heat through. Taste and add more salt and pepper, if needed.

LEFTOVERS:

If you don't eat it all at once, the leftovers will keep for lunch the next day.

CURRIED COUSCOUS PILAF

A classic with some extra veg and flavor boost. If you're not a fan of cauliflower or broccoli, substitute green beans or carrots.

MAKES 4 SERVINGS

1 tablespoon neutral-tasting vegetable oil

1 small onion, minced

1½ cups chopped cauliflower or broccoli

1 tablespoon curry powder

1 cup couscous

¼ teaspoon salt

1 (15.5-ounce) can chickpeas or dark red kidney beans, drained and rinsed

¼ cup frozen green peas, thawed

2 tablespoons raisins or dried cranberries

2 tablespoons unsalted roasted cashews or peanuts

Heat the oil in a large saucepan over medium heat. Add the onion and cauliflower and cook until softened, about 7 minutes. Stir in the curry powder and cook until fragrant, about 30 seconds. Stir in 1¼ cups of water and bring back to a boil. Stir in the couscous and salt and bring to a boil. Add the chickpeas and peas. Cover and remove from the heat. Set aside for 10 minutes, then stir in the raisins and cashews and serve hot.

LEFTOVERS:

Leftovers store well and are even good cold for lunch the next day.

Loaded with goodness

BEANS AND GREENS BURRITOS

Sneak in some extra servings of veggies with these quick, easy, really satisfying burritos.

MAKES 4 SERVINGS

1 tablespoon extra-virgin olive oil

1 medium onion, chopped

1 red bell pepper, chopped

2 cups chopped spinach or kale

1 (15-ounce) can pinto, black, or kidney beans, drained and rinsed

1 cup tomato salsa

Large flour tortillas

Shredded vegan cheese (optional)

Preheat the oven to 275°F.

Heat the olive oil in a saucepan over medium heat. Add the onion and bell pepper, cover, and cook until softened, about 5 minutes. Add the spinach or kale and cook, stirring, for a few minutes longer to soften.

Add the beans and mash them against the side of the saucepan with a fork. Stir in the salsa and cook for 5 minutes to heat through.

Wrap the tortillas in foil and place them in the oven for 5 to 10 minutes to warm.

To serve, spoon about ½ cup of the bean mixture down the center of each tortilla. Top with some cheese, if desired. Fold the sides in over the filling, then roll to enclose. Serve hot.

LEFTOVERS:

This makes enough to fill 4 tortillas and keeps well in the refrigerator or freezer.

SPANISH RICE AND BEANS

Sí sí sí! Serve this hearty classic with a salad for a complete and easy meal. Or get those greens in by stirring in some cooked chopped spinach when you add the beans.

MAKES 2 TO 4 SERVINGS

1 tablespoon extra-virgin olive oil

1 onion, chopped

2 garlic cloves, minced

1 cup long-grain brown rice

1 (14-ounce) can fire-roasted diced tomatoes, undrained

Salt and ground black pepper

1 (15.5-ounce) can dark red kidney beans, drained and rinsed

2 tablespoons minced fresh parsley or cilantro

Heat the olive oil in a large deep skillet or saucepan over medium heat. Add the onion and cook until softened, about 5 minutes. Add the garlic and cook for 1 minute longer. Stir in the rice, then add the tomatoes and their juices, 1½ cups of water, and salt and pepper to taste. Bring to a boil, then reduce the heat to low. Cover and simmer until the rice is tender, about 40 minutes.

Stir in the beans and continue cooking until the rice and vegetables are tender and all the liquid has been absorbed, about 5 minutes longer. Stir in the parsley and serve hot.

wok star

EASY WEEKNIGHT STIR-FRY

The title is no lie. This recipe could not be easier and is loaded with flavor. It calls for frozen stir-fry vegetable mix, but substitute fresh vegetables, if desired. Enjoy on its own, serve over rice or quinoa, or toss with cooked noodles.

MAKES 2 SERVINGS

2 tablespoons neutral-tasting vegetable oil

Choice of vegan protein: 8 ounces extra-firm tofu, well drained and cut into 1-inch cubes; 1½ cups reconstituted Soy Curls; 8 ounces seitan, cut into strips; 8 ounces frozen vegan "chicken" or "beef" strips

2 teaspoons grated fresh ginger

2 garlic cloves, minced

2 cups frozen stir-fry vegetable mix, thawed, or your favorite fresh vegetables cut into bite-size pieces

2 tablespoons soy sauce

1 tablespoon hoisin sauce

1 tablespoon rice vinegar

Heat 1 tablespoon of the oil in a large skillet over medium heat. Add your protein of choice and cook until lightly browned, about 5 minutes. Remove from the skillet and set aside.

Heat the remaining 1 tablespoon oil in the same skillet over medium-high heat. Add the ginger and garlic and cook until fragrant, about 30 seconds. Add the vegetables, soy sauce, and 2 tablespoons of water and stir-fry until the vegetables are cooked and tender, about 8 minutes. Stir in the hoisin sauce and vinegar, then add the reserved vegan protein and stir-fry until heated through, about 5 minutes. Serve hot.

PUTTANESCA PILAF

Jazz up cooked grains with this sassy puttanesca sauce—why should pasta have all the fun?

1 tablespoon extra-virgin olive oil

3 garlic cloves, minced

1 (14.5-ounce) can fire-roasted diced tomatoes, drained

1 (15.5-ounce) can cannellini beans, drained and rinsed

¼ cup sliced pitted Kalamata olives

¼ cup sliced pitted green olives

1 tablespoon capers, drained and chopped

¼ teaspoon red pepper flakes

Salt and ground black pepper

2 cups hot cooked brown rice or quinoa

2 tablespoons minced fresh parsley (optional)

Heat the olive oil in a large skillet over medium heat. Add the garlic and cook, stirring, until fragrant, about 30 seconds. Stir in the tomatoes, beans, olives, capers, pepper flakes, and salt and black pepper to taste. Reduce the heat to low and simmer, stirring occasionally, for 5 minutes to blend the flavors. Add the parsley (if using) and cook, stirring occasionally, to heat through. Serve ladled over rice.

Who needs pasta?

PASTA AND NOODLES

Pasta and White Beans with Creamy Pesto Sauce • 200

Pasta Primavera • 203

Ramen with Spinach and Chickpeas • 204

Penne with Tomato-Mushroom Sauce • 205

Vegetable Lo Mein with Tofu • 206

Noodles with Peanut Sauce • 209

PASTA AND WHITE BEANS WITH CREAMY PESTO SAUCE

We all know pasta with sauce will bring happiness to our tummies, but this flavorful pesto also packs in a protein and fiber punch with the addition of white beans.

MAKES 2 SERVINGS

8 ounces pasta (your favorite)

3 garlic cloves, peeled but whole

½ teaspoon salt

1 (15.5-ounce) can cannellini beans, drained and rinsed

2 cups packed baby spinach

1 cup fresh basil leaves

3 tablespoons extra-virgin olive oil

2 tablespoons nutritional yeast

Halved cherry tomatoes and fresh basil leaves for garnish (optional)

Cook the pasta in a large pot of salted boiling water according to the package directions.

While the pasta is cooking, in a food processor, combine the garlic, salt, and ½ cup of the cannellini beans and process to a coarse paste. Add the spinach, basil, olive oil, and nutritional yeast and process until smooth. Add ¼ cup of the hot pasta cooking water to the pesto and process to combine.

When the pasta is cooked, drain it and return it to the pot. Add the pesto and the remaining cannellini beans to the pasta and toss gently to combine. Taste and add more salt, if needed. Serve hot, garnished with the basil and tomatoes, if you like.

veggie powered

PASTA PRIMAVERA

Pasta tossed with fresh vegetables makes an easy and colorful dinner. For added protein, add a sautéed sliced vegan sausage or some diced tofu or seitan, or cooked or canned chickpeas or cannellini beans.

MAKES 2 OR 3 SERVINGS

8 ounces rotini or other bite-size pasta

2 tablespoons extra-virgin olive oil

1 cup thinly sliced carrot

1 cup small broccoli florets or 1-inch pieces asparagus

3 garlic cloves, minced

2 scallions, chopped

1 cup cherry or grape tomatoes, halved lengthwise

¼ cup frozen green peas, run quickly under hot water to thaw

Salt and ground black pepper

¼ cup chopped fresh basil or parsley

Cook the pasta in a large pot of boiling salted water according to the package directions.

While the pasta is cooking, heat 1 tablespoon of the olive oil in a large skillet over medium heat. Add the carrot and broccoli and cook, stirring, until softened, about 4 minutes. Add the garlic and scallions and cook for 1 minute, then add the tomatoes and peas. Season with salt and pepper and cook for 2 minutes longer, or until the vegetables are tender. Remove from the heat.

Drain the cooked pasta and return it to the pot. Add the sautéed vegetable mixture to the pasta pot. Drizzle on the remaining 1 tablespoon oil and season with salt and pepper to taste. Add the basil and toss to combine. Serve hot.

RAMEN WITH SPINACH AND CHICKPEAS

Get your easy ramen fix here.

Ramen noodles are awesome in this recipe because they cook in just minutes (just throw away the flavoring packet!), but you could easily substitute any leftover grain or pasta. Likewise, baby spinach cooks up in an instant, but you can add your favorite cooked vegetable in its place. And, of course, swap out another type of bean or other vegan protein for the chickpeas, if that's your pleasure. To stretch this to serve three or four, use two bricks of ramen noodles and increase the seasoning for more heat.

MAKES 2 SERVINGS

1 (3-ounce) package ramen noodles (seasoning packet discarded)

1 tablespoon extra-virgin olive oil

2 garlic cloves, minced

1 (9-ounce) bag baby spinach

1 (15.5-ounce) can chickpeas, drained and rinsed

1 (14.5-ounce) can fire-roasted diced tomatoes, drained

2 teaspoons capers (optional), drained

½ teaspoon dried basil

¼ teaspoon red pepper flakes

Salt and ground black pepper

Cook the ramen noodles in boiling water until just tender, 2 to 3 minutes. Drain and set aside.

Heat the olive oil in a skillet over medium heat. Add the garlic and cook, stirring, until softened, about 1 minute. Add the spinach and stir until wilted, about 2 minutes. Add the chickpeas, tomatoes, capers (if using), basil, red pepper flakes, and salt and black pepper to taste. Add the cooked ramen noodles to the skillet and cook for 1 to 2 minutes, tossing to combine and heat through. Serve hot.

PENNE WITH TOMATO-MUSHROOM SAUCE

I mean, yeah, you could use pasta sauce from a jar, but why not make your own in just minutes? The addition of chopped mushrooms provides a meaty texture, but you can substitute vegan burger crumbles (fresh or frozen) instead for the same sensation.

MAKES 2 OR 3 SERVINGS

8 ounces penne or other bite-size pasta

2 tablespoons extra-virgin olive oil

3 garlic cloves, chopped

2 cups chopped mushrooms

1 (28-ounce) can crushed tomatoes

2 teaspoons dried basil

1 teaspoon dried oregano

1 teaspoon dried parsley

¼ teaspoon red pepper flakes (optional)

Salt and ground black pepper

Heat the olive oil in a saucepan over medium heat. Add the garlic and cook until fragrant, about 30 seconds. Stir in the mushrooms and cook until softened, about 4 minutes. Add the tomatoes, basil, oregano, parsley, and red pepper flakes (if using). Season to taste with salt and black pepper and reduce the heat to low. Simmer for 10 minutes, stirring occasionally. Taste and adjust the seasonings, if needed.

While the sauce is simmering, cook the pasta in a pot of boiling salted water according to the package directions.

Drain the pasta and serve topped with the sauce.

VEGETABLE LO MEIN WITH TOFU

Make this Chinese restaurant favorite at home in less time than it takes to pick up takeout—and this version is way healthier and fresher tasting.

MAKES 2 OR 3 SERVINGS

8 ounces spaghetti

1½ cups small broccoli florets

2 teaspoons dark sesame oil

3 tablespoons hoisin sauce

2 tablespoons soy sauce

2 teaspoons rice vinegar

2 tablespoons neutral-tasting vegetable oil

8 ounces extra-firm tofu, drained and cut into ½-inch dice

1 small carrot, shredded or thinly sliced

4 scallions, chopped

2 garlic cloves, minced

½ red bell pepper, cut into thin strips

2 teaspoons grated fresh ginger

Cook the pasta in a pot of boiling salted water according to the package directions. About 4 minutes before the pasta is done, add the broccoli. Drain the pasta and broccoli and return to the pot. Add the sesame oil and toss to coat. Set aside.

While the pasta and broccoli are cooking, in a small bowl, combine the hoisin, soy sauce, vinegar, and ¼ cup of water and stir to blend well.

Heat 1 tablespoon of the vegetable oil in a large skillet over medium-high heat. Add the tofu and stir-fry until lightly browned, about 5 minutes. Transfer the cooked tofu to the pot with the pasta.

Heat the remaining 1 tablespoon vegetable oil in the same skillet. Add the carrot, scallions, and garlic and stir-fry for 3 minutes. Add the bell pepper and ginger and stir-fry for 1 minute longer. Add the sauce and stir-fry to coat. Add the vegetables and sauce to the pot with the noodles and toss until hot.

LEFTOVERS:

This dish tastes even better for lunch the next day!

Better than
takeout

NOODLES WITH PEANUT SAUCE

It's almost not fair to the restaurant version how quick, easy, tasty, and protein-rich this recipe is. If you have fresh veggies, use them in place of the frozen ones. Either way, the stars of the show are the creamy peanut butter sauce and chewy noodles. For a milder version, eliminate or use less of the red pepper flakes.

MAKES 2 OR 3 SERVINGS

8 ounces noodles or linguine

2 cups frozen stir-fry vegetable mix

½ cup creamy peanut butter

3 tablespoons tamari or soy sauce

2 teaspoons fresh lime juice

1 teaspoon light brown sugar

½ teaspoon red pepper flakes

2 tablespoons chopped roasted peanuts

Canned baby corn for garnish (optional)

Cook the noodles and vegetables according to the package directions. When the noodles and vegetables are cooked, drain them in a colander.

While the noodles and vegetables are cooking, make the sauce. In a bowl, whisk together the peanut butter, tamari, lime juice, brown sugar, red pepper flakes, and ½ cup of water. Blend until smooth.

Transfer the peanut sauce to the pot in which the noodles were cooked and stir in as much additional water as needed to give it a smooth, saucy consistency. Place the pot over low heat and warm the sauce, stirring until it is hot. Add the drained noodles and vegetables to the pot and toss gently to coat with the sauce. Heat through until hot. Serve sprinkled with the peanuts. Garnish with the baby corn, if desired.

FROM
THE OVEN

BBQ BAKED TOFU

Baking it with a coating of lip-smacking barbecue sauce is a tasty way to enjoy tofu.

MAKES 4 SERVINGS

14 ounces extra-firm tofu, drained

Salt and ground black pepper

¾ cup barbecue sauce (your favorite), plus more for serving

Cut the tofu into ½-inch-thick slices and arrange them in a single layer on a baking sheet lined with paper towels. Cover with more paper towels and place another baking sheet on top. Place some canned goods on the top baking sheet to weight it down. Let it sit for 20 minutes to press the liquid out of the tofu.

Preheat the oven to 375°F. Line a baking sheet with parchment paper or lightly oil a glass baking dish.

Arrange the pressed tofu slices in a single layer on the prepared baking sheet or baking dish. Season with salt and pepper.

In a small bowl, combine the barbecue sauce with ¼ cup of water, stirring to blend well. Pour about half of the sauce over the tofu, spreading it with the back of a spoon on each slab. Turn the tofu and pour over the remaining sauce, using a spoon to spread the sauce.

Bake until the tofu is browned and nicely glazed with the sauce, turning once about halfway through, about 30 minutes total. Serve hot with additional barbecue sauce.

VARIATION: To give your baked tofu an Asian flavor, omit the barbecue sauce mixture. Instead, in a small bowl, combine ¼ cup tamari, 2 tablespoons fresh lemon juice, 1 tablespoon dark sesame oil, and 1 tablespoon agave nectar. Blend well and pour over the tofu before baking.

QUINOA PINTO LOAF

Old-school meat loaf goes vegan and healthy—and it's way tastier! Top it with Mushroom Gravy (opposite page), and serve with mashed potatoes and roasted vegetables for the ultimate comfort food dinner.

MAKES 4 TO 6 SERVINGS

1 tablespoon ground flax seeds

1 tablespoon extra-virgin olive oil

1 medium onion, minced

2 garlic cloves, minced

1 (15.5-ounce) can pinto beans, drained, rinsed, and blotted dry

1 cup cooked quinoa

1 cup quick-cooking oats (not instant)

½ cup dried breadcrumbs

¼ cup ketchup

1 tablespoon Dijon mustard

¼ cup chopped fresh parsley

1 teaspoon dried thyme

½ teaspoon salt

¼ teaspoon ground black pepper

Mushroom Gravy

In a small bowl, combine 2 tablespoons of warm water and the ground flax seeds and set aside.

Heat the olive oil in a skillet over medium heat. Add the onion and cook until softened, about 5 minutes. Stir in the garlic and cook for 1 minute longer. Remove from the heat and set aside to cool slightly.

Preheat the oven to 350°F. Lightly oil a 9 x 5-inch loaf pan.

Place the beans in a large bowl and mash them well. Add the quinoa, oats, breadcrumbs, sautéed onion mixture, and flax mixture. Stir in the ketchup, mustard, parsley, thyme, salt, and pepper. Mix well to thoroughly combine. Transfer the mixture to the prepared loaf pan, pressing with your hands to smooth it evenly in the pan.

Bake until hot and lightly browned on top, 45 to 50 minutes. Remove from the oven and set aside to cool for 10 minutes before removing from the pan. Slice with a serrated knife. Top with the gravy.

MUSHROOM GRAVY

Meat-based gravy is no match for this mushroom version, which is so much more satisfying. Use this sauce on the Quinoa Pinto Loaf or to top sautéed seitan, mashed potatoes, or even veggie burgers.

MAKES ABOUT 2½ CUPS

1 tablespoon extra-virgin olive oil

1 cup chopped or sliced mushrooms

½ teaspoon onion powder

½ cup all-purpose flour or oat flour

3 tablespoons nutritional yeast

2 cups plain, unsweetened almond or soy milk, plus more as needed

2 tablespoons tamari or soy sauce

Salt and ground black pepper

Heat the olive oil in a saucepan over medium heat. Add the mushrooms and onion powder and cook until the mushrooms are softened, about 5 minutes. Sprinkle on the flour and nutritional yeast, then slowly stir in the milk and the tamari. Continue stirring until smooth and thickened, about 5 minutes. Season with salt and pepper to taste. For a thinner sauce, stir in a little more soy or nondairy milk. Serve hot.

SPINACH LASAGNA

Want to impress your friends or your folks? Here you go, and you're welcome. This is a main dish that will please everyone. Make this in a large pan for several people, but if you want to keep it all for yourself (and I don't blame you), divide the ingredients among two or even three smaller baking dishes, cutting the lasagna noodles to fit; then cover one or two dishes tightly and freeze for another time.

MAKES 4 TO 6 SERVINGS

12 lasagna noodles

1 (15.5-ounce) can white beans, drained and rinsed

14 ounces firm tofu, drained

½ cup nutritional yeast

¼ cup chopped fresh parsley

1 teaspoon fresh or dried basil

½ teaspoon dried oregano

½ teaspoon onion powder

¼ teaspoon garlic powder

Salt and ground black pepper

1 (10-ounce) package frozen chopped spinach, thawed and squeezed dry

1 (28-ounce) jar marinara sauce

1 cup shredded vegan cheese (optional)

Place the noodles in a shallow 9 x 13-inch baking dish and pour on enough boiling salted water to cover. Set aside while you make the filling. Preheat the oven to 350°F.

In a large bowl, combine the beans, tofu, nutritional yeast, parsley, basil, oregano, onion powder, garlic powder, 1 teaspoon salt, and ½ teaspoon pepper. Mash with a potato masher until smooth and well combined. Add the spinach and mix well, then taste and adjust the seasoning, adding more salt if needed.

Drain the noodles and spread them in a single layer on a plate or a piece of plastic wrap. Spread a layer of the marinara sauce in the bottom of the baking dish and place 3 noodles on top of the sauce, overlapping them slightly. Spread half the filling mixture over the noodles, then top with 3 more noodles. Spread a thin layer of sauce on top and spread the remaining filling mixture over it. Top with the remaining 3 noodles and spread the remaining sauce over the noodles. Sprinkle the top with cheese (if using).

Cover with aluminum foil and bake until hot, 45 to 50 minutes. Let stand for 10 to 15 minutes before serving.

PIZZA AS YOU LIKE IT

Because, pizza. And did you know how easy (and fun) it is to make your own?

For convenience, make your pizza dough well ahead of time. This recipe makes enough for two large pizzas. If you're making only one pizza, freeze the other dough ball for a future pizza. Just be sure to take it out of the freezer a few hours before needed so it can thaw at room temperature. If you prefer not to make your own dough, you can buy ready-made pizza dough in the refrigerated case of most supermarkets. I like the Trader Joe's brand.

MAKES 2 (10-INCH) PIZZAS

Dough:

1 envelope (2½ teaspoons) rapid rise active dry yeast

1 teaspoon sugar

1½ cups warm water (110°F)

2 tablespoons extra-virgin olive oil, plus more for brushing crust

3 cups all-purpose flour, plus more for kneading

1 teaspoon salt

Toppings:

Pizza sauce or marinara sauce (your favorite)

½ teaspoon dried oregano

Shredded vegan mozzarella

Your choice of sliced mushrooms or other sautéed vegetables (see Chef's Tip); sliced pitted Kalamata olives; sliced artichoke hearts; or sliced vegan pepperoni

Make the dough:

In a small bowl, combine the yeast, sugar, water, and 2 tablespoons of olive oil. Stir to combine and set aside for 5 minutes to activate the yeast.

In a food processor, pulse together the flour and salt to combine. With the machine running, pour in the yeast mixture. Process until the dough forms a ball on the blades. (If not using a food processor, stir the flour and salt together in a large bowl. Add the yeast mixture and stir with a large spoon to form a dough, then use your hands to knead it into a ball.)

Transfer the dough ball to a lightly floured surface and knead it for about 2 minutes, adding flour as necessary, until it is smooth and elastic. Transfer the dough to a lightly oiled bowl, turning to coat with the oil. Cover the bowl tightly with plastic wrap and set it in a warm spot to rise for 1 hour.

Turn the dough out onto a lightly floured surface and divide it into two equal pieces. Roll each dough ball around under your palm until the ball feels smooth and firm, about 1 minute. Put the balls on a plate, cover with plastic wrap, and set aside to rest for at least 30 minutes. (Alternatively, the dough can be covered with plastic wrap and refrigerated for up to 48 hours.)

Place the oven rack in the lowest position in the oven. Preheat the oven to 450°F.

Place one of the dough balls on a lightly floured surface, punching it to deflate. To shape the dough, press down on its center with the heel of your hand while turning the dough, gradually spreading it out to a round about 10 inches in diameter. (Alternatively, use a rolling pin to create an even round.) With your fingers, form a slightly thicker raised rim around the edge of the pizza. Transfer the pizza to a lightly oiled pizza pan.

Brush the surface of the dough with a little olive oil.

Top the pizza:
Spread a thin layer of pizza sauce or marinara sauce over the dough up to within ½ inch of the rim all around. Sprinkle with the oregano. Top with shredded cheese. If desired, top with the mushrooms, olives, artichoke hearts, or vegan pepperoni.

Transfer the pizza to the oven and bake until the rim of the crust is deep golden brown, 12 to 14 minutes. While the pizza bakes, roll out and top the second pizza.

Transfer the pizza to a cutting board. Use a pizza cutter or a sharp knife to cut the pizza into slices and serve immediately.

CHEF'S TIP
It's always best to use cooked vegetables to top your pizza, as raw veggies may exude juices that will make your pizza soggy.

Mmmm... Brussels sprouts

ROASTED VEGETABLE BAKE

There's no shortage of nutrients and delicious flavor in this simple and hearty veg casserole. Mix and match the vegetables according to taste, or swap in a different vegetable such as sliced or cubed butternut squash. The recipe is easily doubled. To make this a one-dish meal, add some sautéed seitan or tempeh or cooked beans a few minutes before the vegetables are done cooking.

MAKES 2 SERVINGS

1 medium red onion, cut into ½-inch pieces

1 large carrot, cut into ¼-inch slices

1 Yukon Gold potato, well scrubbed and cut into 1-inch chunks

1 cup Brussels sprouts, trimmed and halved

1 cup small cauliflower florets

1 tablespoon tamari or soy sauce

1 tablespoon pure maple syrup

1 tablespoon rice vinegar

1 tablespoon extra-virgin olive oil

1 teaspoon Dijon mustard

1 teaspoon dried thyme

Salt and ground black pepper

Preheat the oven to 400°F. Lightly oil a shallow 9 x 12-inch baking dish.

Arrange the vegetables in the dish in a single layer. In a small bowl, combine the tamari, maple syrup, vinegar, olive oil, mustard, and thyme and stir to blend. Stir in 3 tablespoons of water and pour the mixture over the vegetables. Season to taste with salt and pepper.

Cover the baking dish tightly with aluminum foil and bake for 30 minutes. Remove the foil and stir the vegetables gently. Return the dish to the oven and continue baking, uncovered, until the vegetables are tender when pierced with a fork, about 20 minutes longer. Serve hot.

MAC 'N' CHEESE, PLEASE

This creamy, satisfying mac and cheese is the ultimate comfort food, and it's so easy to make! If you don't have panko or other breadcrumbs on hand, crush some potato chips for a crunchy (and tasty!) topping.

MAKES 4 SERVINGS

8 ounces elbow macaroni or other bite-size pasta

½ cup raw cashews, soaked 4 hours in water to cover, drained

3 cups plain, unsweetened almond milk

⅓ cup jarred roasted red pepper

2 tablespoons fresh lemon juice

1 teaspoon Dijon mustard

½ cup nutritional yeast

2 tablespoons cornstarch

1 teaspoon salt

1 teaspoon onion powder

1 teaspoon smoked paprika (optional)

¼ teaspoon ground black pepper

3 tablespoons panko breadcrumbs or crushed potato chips

Preheat the oven to 375°F. Lightly oil a 9-inch square baking dish.

Cook the macaroni in a pot of boiling salted water until it is al dente. Drain and return to the pot.

In a blender or food processor, combine the drained cashews and 1 cup of the almond milk and puree until smooth. Add the roasted red pepper, lemon juice, mustard, nutritional yeast, cornstarch, salt, onion powder, smoked paprika (if using), and pepper. Add the remaining 2 cups almond milk and blend until completely smooth and creamy.

Add the sauce mixture to the drained macaroni and stir to combine. Taste and add more salt and pepper if needed. Transfer the mixture to the prepared baking dish and sprinkle with the panko. Bake until bubbling and golden brown on top, 20 to 30 minutes.

Lose the box

SHORTCUT SHEPHERD'S PIE

Shepherd's pie is at the top of the comfort food list, and here it's been veganized and made easy. Frozen mixed vegetables shorten the prep time, and you can put the entire dish together ahead of time (even the night before) and pop it in the oven when needed. You'll just need to bake it a little longer to heat through if it has been refrigerated.

MAKES 6 SERVINGS

1½ pounds russet or other baking potatoes (2 large potatoes)

½ cup plain, unsweetened almond milk or soy milk

2 tablespoons vegan butter (such as Earth Balance brand)

1 tablespoon nutritional yeast

Salt and ground black pepper

2 cups frozen mixed vegetables (peas, carrots, and corn), microwaved or steamed until tender

1 tablespoon extra-virgin olive oil

1 medium onion, finely chopped

1½ cups chopped mushrooms

1 (15.5-ounce) can lentils or navy beans, drained and rinsed, or thawed frozen vegan burger crumbles

2 cups Mushroom Gravy (page 215)

Preheat the oven to 400°F. Lightly oil a 9-inch square baking dish.

Peel the potatoes and cut them into 1-inch chunks. Steam them in a steamer basket over boiling water until tender, about 15 minutes. Drain and transfer to a large bowl. Add the almond milk, butter, nutritional yeast, and salt and pepper to taste and mash until smooth. Set aside.

Heat the olive oil in a large skillet over medium heat. Add the onion and cook until softened, about 5 minutes. Add the mushrooms and cook until softened. Season with salt and pepper to taste. Stir in the cooked mixed vegetables and the lentils or other protein. Stir in the gravy and mix well.

Spread the filling evenly in the prepared dish, then cover completely with the mashed potatoes. Bake until the potatoes are slightly browned, about 30 minutes. Serve hot.

TORTILLA BAKE

Everything everyone loves in one main dish. This tasty recipe is easily doubled or tripled for a crowd.

MAKES 3 OR 4 SERVINGS

1 (15.5-ounce) can pinto beans, drained and rinsed

½ teaspoon chili powder, or more to taste

¼ teaspoon dried oregano

¼ teaspoon ground cumin

1 (16-ounce) jar tomato salsa (hot or mild)

6 small (6-inch) flour tortillas

1 cup nacho cheese sauce (from Nachos for Dinner, page 186) or shredded vegan cheddar

Salt and ground black pepper

Place the beans in a large bowl and coarsely mash them. Add the chili powder, oregano, cumin, and 2 tablespoons of water and mash until incorporated. Stir in 1 cup of the salsa and mix until combined.

Preheat the oven to 350°F. Lightly oil an 8-inch square baking dish.

Spread a thin layer of the remaining salsa on the bottom of the baking dish. Arrange 3 tortillas on top of the salsa, overlapping them as necessary. Spread the bean mixture evenly over the tortillas in the baking dish, then top with the remaining tortillas, pressing lightly. Spread the remaining salsa over the tortillas and drizzle with the nacho sauce or sprinkle with the cheese.

Cover tightly with aluminum foil and bake until hot and bubbling, about 30 minutes. Remove from the oven and let stand about 10 minutes before serving.

Serve hot.

BAKED POTATO BAR

A baked potato loaded with toppings is an easy, delicious, and economical meal whether you're cooking for yourself or the whole gang. Go with classic russets or other baking potato, or try sweet potatoes. Better yet, bake some of both!

This recipe is more of a guideline than an actual recipe, since the amount of potatoes you bake and number of toppings you prepare is up to you.

1 large russet (baking) potato or sweet potato per person, well scrubbed and dried

Extra-virgin olive oil

Salt and ground black pepper

Toppings (as many or as few as you wish):

Vegan butter

Vegan sour cream

Shredded vegan cheddar cheese

Nacho cheese sauce (from Nachos for Dinner, page 186), warmed

BBQ Black Bean Chili (page 149), warmed

Cooked beans (any kind), warmed

Vegan bacon bits

Diced seitan, BBQ tempeh, sliced vegan sausage, warmed

Chopped scallions, chives, or fresh herbs

Sautéed or caramelized onions, warmed

Cooked chopped broccoli or kale

Sautéed bell peppers, mushrooms, or spinach, warmed

Guacamole or mashed Hass avocado

Chopped tomatoes

Sliced pitted Kalamata olives

Roasted pumpkin seeds, sunflower seeds, or chopped walnuts

Pesto

Salsa

Sriracha or other hot sauce

Nut butter or tahini

Barbecue sauce

Preheat the oven to 425°F.

Rub the potato skins with olive oil and sprinkle with salt and pepper. Use a fork to pierce each potato in a few places. Arrange the potatoes on a baking sheet and bake until a knife can be easily inserted into the potatoes, 50 minutes to 1 hour.

While the potatoes are baking, prepare your toppings of choice. (This is a great way to use up small amounts of leftovers!)

To serve, cut into each baked potato lengthwise about halfway through, then push the potato from the sides to expose the flesh inside. Load up your potatoes with as many or as few toppings as you like.

LEFTOVERS:

If you have leftover potatoes, slice and sauté them for dinner the next night with salt, pepper, oregano, and a squeeze of lemon juice, or mash them up and use them as a topping for the Shortcut Shepherd's Pie (page 224). You can always just warm up a leftover baked potato in the microwave, split it open, and load on some toppings for round two the next day.

SNACKS

Betcha can't
have just one
(handful)

JERK-SPICED ROASTED CHICKPEAS

You won't believe how amazingly delicious chickpeas can be as a snack. And they're so cheap and easy to make! If you prefer not to use the jerk seasoning, you can make them plain, or with just a little salt, or season them however you like. Throw 'em into your mouth like popcorn, or add them to a salad.

MAKES 4 SERVINGS

1 (15.5-ounce) can chickpeas, drained, rinsed, and blotted dry

2 tablespoons extra-virgin olive oil

Salt

2 teaspoons jerk seasoning

Preheat the oven to 400°F. Lightly oil a shallow baking pan or rimmed baking sheet or coat it with cooking spray.

Spread the chickpeas in a single layer in the prepared pan and drizzle with the olive oil. Toss gently to coat. Season with salt to taste.

Roast the chickpeas, stirring occasionally, until they begin to brown and turn crispy, about 30 minutes. Remove from the oven and sprinkle on the jerk spices and a little more salt, if needed. Cool to room temperature.

CLASSIC HUMMUS

Serve with chips for a high-protein snack, or spread on a veggie sandwich.

MAKES ABOUT 2 CUPS

1 (15.5-ounce) can chickpeas, drained and rinsed

2 garlic cloves, crushed

½ teaspoon salt

3 tablespoons tahini

2 tablespoons fresh lemon juice

Chopped fresh parsley, for garnish (optional)

Set a handful of whole chickpeas aside for garnish. Transfer the rest to a food processor and add the garlic and salt. Puree to a paste. Add the tahini and lemon juice and process until smooth and completely blended, scraping down the sides a few times.

Transfer the hummus to a shallow bowl. Cover and refrigerate for 1 hour to allow the flavors to develop. Serve chilled or at room temperature, garnished with the reserved chickpeas and chopped parsley, if desired.

VARIATIONS:

Low-Cal Hummus: Substitute water for the tahini.

Roasted Garlic Hummus: Replace the raw garlic with 1 whole bulb garlic, roasted, the cloves squeezed out of their skins.

Hot 'n' Spicy Hummus: Add 1 tablespoon of Sriracha or chipotle chile in adobo to the recipe.

Roasted Red Pepper Hummus: Add ¼ to ⅓ cup chopped jarred roasted red pepper.

Sun-Dried Tomato Hummus: Add 2 tablespoons minced oil-packed or reconstituted dry-packed sun-dried tomatoes.

Spice It Up Hummus: Add ½ teaspoon each ground cumin and smoked paprika.

Make it
your way

SUPER GUAC

Gimme gimme gimme that guac! This one has some extra goodies, such as bits of onion and tomato sharing the bowl with the avocado. In addition to making the ultimate dip for tortilla chips, guacamole is a fantastic topping for tacos, chili, salads, and more. You can even thin it out with a little plain, unsweetened almond or soy milk and use it as a sauce for pasta—just be sure to eat it on the same day you make it because it will turn brown after an hour or so.

MAKES 4 SERVINGS

2 Hass avocados, halved and pitted

1 tablespoon fresh lime juice

¼ teaspoon salt

1 plum tomato, finely chopped

2 tablespoons minced red onion

2 tablespoons minced fresh cilantro

1 jalapeño, seeded and minced (optional)

Scoop the avocado flesh into a bowl. Add the lime juice and salt and mash everything together. Stir in the tomato, onion, cilantro, and jalapeño (if using). Taste and add more salt or lime juice if needed. If not serving right away, cover with plastic wrap, pressing the wrap directly onto the surface of the guac to keep it from discoloring, and refrigerate for up to 8 hours.

VARIATION: To stretch the guac (and add more nutrients and flavor at the same time), stir in ½ cup canned black beans (drained and rinsed) and ⅓ cup bottled green salsa (salsa verde).

SUPERFOOD TRAIL MIX

Why settle for someone else's version of trail mix when you can make your own? Explore the bulk section of your supermarket and put together your own custom blend. Be sure to include sweet and savory flavors and soft and crunchy textures to make it more fun to munch. Adding superfoods like goji berries, dried blueberries, and nuts will make it superhealthy, too. Seal it in airtight sandwich bags and keep in a cool spot. It will stay fresh for several days. This recipe can be easily halved or doubled. Happy trails!

MAKES ABOUT 4 CUPS

½ cup pistachios

½ cup cashews, almonds, or walnuts

½ cup roasted sunflower seeds or pumpkin seeds

½ cup dried blueberries

½ cup dried cranberries

½ cup goji berries (or more dried cranberries)

½ cup cacao nibs or vegan chocolate chips

½ cup mini pretzels

In a large bowl, combine all the ingredients and toss gently to combine. Divide the mixture into four resealable sandwich-size plastic bags. Store in a cool, dry place.

SIMPLY STUFFED CELERY

Celery stuffed with nut butter is a sneaky-good combo. There are lots of ways to play with the basic two-ingredient classic: Turn it into "ants on a log" by adding raisins, or use a different kind of nut butter beyond the traditional peanut. This version features almond butter and a topping of sunflower seeds. Use whatever type of sunflower seeds you prefer: roasted or raw, salted or unsalted.

MAKES 4 SERVINGS

5 or 6 celery stalks, ends and leaved trimmed

½ cup almond butter, at room temperature

½ cup sunflower seeds

Use a vegetable peeler or sharp paring knife to remove a thin strip lengthwise from the curved back of each celery stalk so they lie flat without wobbling.

Use a butter knife to fill each celery stalk with almond butter. Place the sunflower seeds in a shallow bowl and dip the stuffed celery into the sunflower seeds, almond butter–side down. Gently press the seeds into the nut butter, if needed. Cut each stalk into 1-inch-long pieces. Arrange on a plate and serve.

PEANUT BUTTER AND CRANBERRY PROTEIN BARS

Flip the bird to the high cost of protein bars by making them yourself. Then you can also customize them to include all your favorite ingredients. And freshly made is always tastier!

MAKES 8 (2 X 4-INCH) BARS

¾ cup walnut pieces (or other type of nut)

1¼ cups old-fashioned rolled oats (not quick-cooking or instant)

1 cup dried cranberries or other dried fruit (or a combination)

½ cup vegan semisweet chocolate chips

½ cup pure maple syrup

3 tablespoons peanut butter

1 tablespoon vegan butter, melted

1 teaspoon vanilla extract

Preheat the oven to 375°F. Grease an 8-inch square baking pan.

Place the walnuts in a dry skillet and toast over medium heat until light brown and fragrant, 3 to 4 minutes, shaking often. Transfer them to a food processor.

Add the remaining ingredients to the food processor and pulse until crumbly. Continue to process until the mixture is well combined. Add a little water, a tablespoon at a time, if the mixture is too crumbly to stick together. Press the mixture evenly into the prepared pan.

Bake until lightly browned, about 20 minutes. Remove from the oven and set aside to cool, then refrigerate until completely cold. Cut into 2 x 4-inch bars. Wrap each bar individually in plastic wrap for easy transport.

ARTICHOKE AND WHITE BEAN SPREAD

Mouthwateringly delicious. Serve on crackers or crusty bread, or use it as a dip with carrot and celery sticks.

MAKES ABOUT 2 CUPS

1 (15.5-ounce) can cannellini beans or other white beans, drained and rinsed

1 (6-ounce) jar marinated artichoke hearts, drained

1 garlic clove, chopped

1 tablespoon capers, drained

2 tablespoons fresh lemon juice

Salt and ground black pepper, to taste

In a food processor, combine all the ingredients and blend until nearly smooth, scraping down the sides with a rubber spatula once or twice. If you want it smoother, add a little water, 1 tablespoon at a time, and continue to process until smooth and creamy. Transfer to a bowl. Cover and refrigerate until ready to serve, up to 3 days.

BLACK BEAN DIP

Did someone say party? Serve this delicious, protein-packed dip with tortilla chips or raw veggies. You can also spread it on a tortilla as a flavorful base for a wrap (just add veggies). If you don't like it spicy, leave out the chipotle chile.

MAKES ABOUT 2 CUPS

2 garlic cloves, crushed

1 (15.5-ounce) can black beans, drained and rinsed

1 canned chipotle chile in adobo sauce

2 tablespoons almond butter

2 tablespoons fresh lime juice

½ teaspoon smoked paprika (optional)

½ teaspoon ground coriander

½ teaspoon ground cumin

Salt and ground black pepper

2 tablespoons chopped fresh cilantro

In a food processor, combine the garlic, black beans, and chipotle and process to a paste. Add the almond butter, lime juice, smoked paprika (if using), coriander, cumin, and ⅓ cup of water and blend until smooth and creamy. Season with salt and pepper to taste. Add 1 tablespoon of the cilantro and pulse to combine. Transfer the dip to a bowl, sprinkle with the remaining cilantro, and serve.

CRUNCH-TIME POPCORN

Pop some serious flavor. This popcorn is deliciously addictive thanks to the cheesy flavor of nutritional yeast (which also—surprise!—provides vitamin B12). The optional sunflower seeds add extra crunch and protein.

MAKES ABOUT 4 CUPS

1 tablespoon grapeseed or coconut oil

½ cup unpopped popcorn kernels

3 tablespoons nutritional yeast

1 teaspoon salt

¼ cup roasted sunflower seeds (optional)

Heat the oil in a heavy-bottomed medium sauce-pan over high heat. Add the popcorn kernels and shake the pan so the kernels are in a single layer. Put on the lid. The kernels will soon begin to pop. When they do, shake the pan frequently to move the kernels around and prevent burning. As soon as the popcorn is done popping, immediately pour it into a large bowl and sprinkle with the nutritional yeast, salt, and sunflower seeds (if using).

BUFFALO CAULIFLOWER BITES

Watch the game and trade in the chicken wings for this supertasty and nutrient-rich roasted cauliflower version slathered in hot sauce and dipped in ranch dressing.

MAKES 4 TO 6 SERVINGS

1 head cauliflower, trimmed and cored

Extra-virgin olive oil or cooking spray

Salt and ground black pepper

Ranch dressing:

½ cup canned cannellini or other white beans

¼ cup vegan mayonnaise

2 tablespoons cider vinegar

¼ teaspoon onion powder

¼ teaspoon garlic powder

¼ teaspoon celery salt

Hot sauce:

⅓ cup Frank's RedHot Cayenne Pepper Sauce

¼ cup vegan butter (such as Earth Balance brand)

1 tablespoon rice vinegar (optional)

Preheat the oven to 425°F. Lightly oil a large rimmed baking sheet or coat it with cooking spray.

Cut the cauliflower into small florets and arrange them in the pan. Drizzle with a little olive oil or spray with a bit of cooking spray. Season with salt and pepper to taste and roast until just tender and nicely browned, 15 to 20 minutes, turning the cauliflower with a spatula once about halfway through.

Meanwhile, make the ranch dressing:
While the cauliflower roasts, combine the dressing ingredients in a food processor and process until smooth. Taste and adjust the seasonings, if needed. Set aside.

Make the hot sauce:
Heat the hot sauce ingredients in a small saucepan, stirring until the butter melts and the sauce is hot.

Pour the hot sauce over the roasted cauliflower, turning to coat. Return the cauliflower to the oven. Bake for about 15 minutes longer. Serve hot with the ranch sauce for dipping.

DESSERT

Fresh Peach and Blueberry Crisp • 249

Chocolate Chippers • 250

Chocolate-Almond Banana Soft-Serve • 252

Chocolate Mug Cake • 253

Stuffed Baked Apples • 255

Chocolate Truffles • 256

No-Bake Date-Nut Cookies • 259

À la mode Me

FRESH PEACH AND BLUEBERRY CRISP

Bedazzle your summer fruit with this delish-but-not-so-decadent treat. (Or you could make it max decadent by topping it with vegan vanilla ice cream.)

MAKES 4 TO 6 SERVINGS

Topping:

⅔ cup old-fashioned rolled oats (not quick-cooking or instant)

⅔ cup packed light brown sugar

¼ cup all-purpose flour

¾ teaspoon ground cinnamon

⅛ teaspoon salt

¼ cup vegan butter, cut into small pieces

Filling:

⅓ cup packed light brown sugar

1½ teaspoons cornstarch

1 tablespoon fresh lemon juice

¼ teaspoon vanilla extract

2 pounds ripe peaches (5 medium peaches), pitted and cut into ½-inch-thick slices

½ cup blueberries

Preheat the oven to 425°F. Lightly grease an 8-inch square baking dish or coat it with cooking spray.

Make the topping:

In a medium bowl, combine the topping ingredients and mix well, using your fingertips to blend the butter into the dry ingredients just until incorporated and crumbly. Set aside.

Make the filling:

In a large bowl, whisk together the brown sugar, cornstarch, lemon juice, and vanilla. Add the peaches and stir until evenly coated. Fold in the blueberries.

Transfer the fruit mixture to the prepared baking dish, spreading it evenly. Sprinkle the topping evenly over the fruit. Bake until the topping is browned and crisp, about 20 minutes. Cool the crisp for at least 20 minutes before serving.

CHOCOLATE CHIPPERS

Want. Chocolate. Chip. Cookies. NOW!

Everyone needs a recipe for chocolate chip cookies for those times when only chocolate chip cookies will do! And this veganized take is way easier and healthier than the traditional version.

MAKES ABOUT 2 DOZEN

1 cup all-purpose flour

½ teaspoon baking powder

⅛ teaspoon salt

¼ cup packed light brown sugar

¼ cup pure maple syrup

1 tablespoon safflower oil

2 tablespoons plain, unsweetened nondairy milk

½ teaspoon vanilla extract

½ cup semisweet vegan chocolate chips

Preheat the oven to 350°F. Lightly oil a baking sheet or line it with parchment paper and set aside.

In a medium bowl, combine the flour, baking powder, and salt. In a large bowl, stir together the brown sugar, maple syrup, oil, nondairy milk, and vanilla until well blended. Add the flour mixture to the wet ingredients and mix until just combined. Stir in the chocolate chips.

Drop the dough by the spoonful about 2 inches apart onto the prepared baking sheet. Bake until golden brown, about 15 minutes. Cool on the pan for 10 minutes, then transfer to a wire rack to cool completely before storing in an airtight container for up to 1 week.

CHOCOLATE-ALMOND BANANA SOFT-SERVE

Food hack alert! Processing frozen banana pieces makes a delicious ready-to-eat ice cream, even without an ice cream maker. Throw in some chocolate and almond butter for extra goodness.

MAKES 2 SERVINGS

2 ripe bananas, peeled, quartered, and frozen

½ teaspoon almond extract (optional)

2 tablespoons almond butter, at room temperature

⅓ cup vegan semisweet mini chocolate chips

Place the frozen banana pieces in a food processor and process until smooth, 3 to 4 minutes, stopping occasionally to scrape down the sides with a rubber spatula. When the bananas are almost but not completely smooth, add the almond extract (if using), almond butter, and chocolate chips. Continue to blend until the bananas are smooth and the other ingredients are incorporated. Transfer to two bowls and enjoy.

> VARIATIONS: Use a different extract to replace the almond extract; omit the chocolate chips; fold in fresh fruit or nuts just before serving.

CHOCOLATE MUG CAKE

This is the answer to those late-night chocolate cravings—your own individual warm chocolate cake, ready in just minutes.

¼ cup all-purpose flour

¼ cup sugar

2 tablespoons unsweetened cocoa powder

2 tablespoons safflower oil

In a large microwave-safe mug, combine the flour, sugar, and cocoa. Mix well. Stir in the oil and 2 tablespoons of water and mix to combine thoroughly. Place the mug in the microwave and cook on high for 45 seconds to 1 minute (or a few seconds longer, depending on your microwave). The cake should still be somewhat wet in the center when done. Let cool for 3 to 5 minutes before digging in.

Fall favorites

STUFFED BAKED APPLES

Cheat on apple pie with this sweet but healthy apple treat. Amp it up with some vegan vanilla ice cream on top.

MAKES 2 SERVINGS

3 tablespoons all-purpose flour

3 tablespoons old-fashioned rolled oats (not quick-cooking or instant)

¼ cup packed light brown sugar

⅛ teaspoon salt

½ teaspoon ground cinnamon

3 tablespoons cold vegan butter, cut into cubes

2 tablespoons chopped pecans

2 tablespoons pure maple syrup

1 teaspoon fresh lemon juice

2 large Gala or Fuji apples

Preheat the oven to 400°F.

In a medium bowl, combine the flour, oats, brown sugar, salt, and cinnamon. Cut in the butter with a fork or use your hands to rub the ingredients together until the mixture is crumbly. Mix in the pecans, maple syrup, and lemon juice and set aside.

Slice the tops off of the apples and use a spoon to scoop out the seeds and enough of the flesh in the center to make a well for the filling. Spoon the filling mixture into the scooped-out apples, pressing gently to pack it in. Place the stuffed apples in a small baking dish and top them with any remaining filling mixture.

Bake until the apples are softened and the topping is crispy, about 20 minutes. Serve warm.

CHOCOLATE TRUFFLES

These sophisticated little treats are easy to make and delicious to eat. They also make a great gift; place them in little paper candy cups and arrange in a small box to really impress. (Or eat them all yourself. I'm not judging.)

MAKES ABOUT 18

1 cup vegan semisweet chocolate chips

½ cup plain, unsweetened almond milk

½ tablespoon vegan butter or coconut oil, melted

Unsweetened cocoa powder, for rolling

Place the chocolate chips in a heatproof bowl. Heat the almond milk in a small saucepan and bring just to a boil, then immediately pour it over the chocolate chips. Let it sit for about 1 minute and then stir until the chocolate has melted and the mixture is well combined and smooth. Stir in the melted butter and set aside to cool to room temperature. Cover and refrigerate for 4 hours or overnight.

Line a baking sheet with waxed paper or parchment paper. Scoop about ½ tablespoon of the chocolate mixture at a time and use your hands to shape it into 1-inch balls. Arrange the balls on the prepared baking sheet. Place the baking sheet in the refrigerator for about 10 minutes to chill the truffles.

Place the cocoa in a shallow bowl. Roll the balls between your hands to make them perfectly round, then roll each one in the cocoa. Return the truffles to the fridge for another 15 minutes to firm up, or cover and store in the fridge for up to 1 week.

It's date night

NO-BAKE DATE-NUT COOKIES

No flour. No sugar. No bake. Yes to tasty treats!

MAKES ABOUT 2 DOZEN

2 cups soft Medjool dates, pitted

2 cups chopped walnuts or pecans, plus more for decorating, if desired

1 cup unsweetened shredded coconut

2 tablespoons coconut oil, melted

1 teaspoon vanilla extract

1 teaspoon salt

In a food processor, combine the dates, nuts, and coconut and process until crumbly. Add the coconut oil, vanilla, and salt and process until it forms a sticky dough. Scoop the dough by heaping tablespoons, rolling it between your palms to form balls. Arrange them on a baking sheet lined with parchment paper, pressing down to flatten slightly. You can press a piece of walnut or pecan in the top center of the cookies, if you like. Refrigerate the pan of cookies for at least 3 hours to firm up before serving. Store any leftover cookies in a sealed container in the fridge for up to a week.

GLOSSARY

Agar: A vegan substitute for gelatin, it's a clear seaweed that's used as a thickener and in baking.

Agave nectar: A natural sweetener made from the agave plant, it's often used as a substitute for honey or sugar.

Amino acids: These organic compounds are the building blocks of protein. They help build the muscular structure of the body and help process the body's cellular functions.

Arrowroot: A fine white powder used to thicken sauces and desserts.

Bean curd: Another name for tofu.

Edamame: Young, green soybeans. You can find them frozen in the pod or shelled, and occasionally fresh in the produce section. They make great snacks or can be added to veggie stir-fries. (But don't eat the pods!)

Food co-op: A food store or food distribution outlet organized by its own members, who often work there in return for lower prices.

Gluten: A general term for the proteins found in wheat, rye, and barley.

GMO (genetically modified organism): Foods produced from organisms that have had specific changes made to their DNA through genetic engineering.

Hemp seed: A source of protein, hemp seeds come from certain varieties of the cannabis plant. Add hemp seeds to salads, cereals, smoothies, desserts, breads, pancakes, granola bars, and other baked goods. BTW, hemp seeds do not contain THC (tetrahydrocannabinol), the psychoactive substance in marijuana.

Legumes: A food plant contained within a seed or a pod. Peas, beans, peanuts, and alfalfa are all legumes, as are chickpeas and lentils.

Nori: Crisp sheets of edible seaweed often used in Japanese cooking. You can use it to make sushi rolls or wraps with rice, veggies, avocado, and/or tofu.

Nutritional yeast: An inactive yeast with a savory, cheesy flavor. It's vegan, gluten-free, and available in most health food stores, and is also a rich source of B vitamins, protein, selenium, and zinc.

Organic: Food produced without the use of pesticides and synthetic fertilizers.

Seitan: A replacement for meat made of the protein (gluten) extracted from wheat.

Tempeh: A dense, firm meat substitute made from soybeans, water, rice or another grain, and a fermenting agent. Because it's fermented, it's supereasy to digest. You can stir-fry it in bite-size pieces with veggies, grill or blacken a slab of it to be the protein center of a meal, or crumble it up and use it like ground beef in a pasta or casserole.

Tofu: A great protein source that's made from soy milk curds pressed into blocks. It comes in different forms that make it superversatile; use *extra-firm* for frying, baking, grilling, marinating; *firm* for stir-frying, boiling, filling; *soft* or *silken* (smooth, vacuum-packed) for pureeing, simmering, or as egg substitute.

TVP (textured vegetable protein): A highly processed replacement for meat, it's a by-product of soybean oil extraction. Also known as TSP, or textured soy protein. Use it as you would ground beef, but sparingly, since it's so processed.

GRRR, ANIMAL STUFF IS LURKING EVERYWHERE!

Not to make you crazy, but be aware of this sneaky stuff and avoid it if you can. Read food labels carefully!

CASEIN: A milk protein sometimes found in protein powders and processed foods such as soy creamer and soy cheeses. (Not so) fun fact: Casein is used in labs to make cancer cells grow. Cornell University's Professor Emeritus of Nutritional Bio-chemistry, T. Colin Campbell, says that in his decades of cancer research, he has found that *casein*, "which makes up 87% of cow's milk protein, promoted all stages of the *cancer* process."

GELATIN: A food product made by boiling the skin, bones, and protective tissue of cattle, horses, and pigs, gelatin is often used to solidify liquids (for instance, Jell-O). Many processed foods and candies contain gelatin.

LACTIC ACID: A food preservative and flavoring agent. Often an ingredient in processed foods, it's also used as a decontaminant during meat processing. An acid ingredient of sour dairy products, fermented fruits and vegetables, and sausages.

RENNET: An enzyme from the stomach of slaughtered calves that's found in many but not all cheeses—even some that call themselves "nondairy."

SHOPPING LIST

Here's a shopping list to make a well-stocked kitchen. Everyone's needs and budgets are different, so use this as a starting place and build your pantry gradually as more and more of your meals are vegan. Don't feel you need to buy everything at once; and you certainly don't need everything.

STAPLES
- Nondairy milk such as soy, rice, hemp, or nut (almond, cashew, etc.). Try a bunch to figure out which you like best. Avoid sweetened or flavored varieties; they just contain extra calories.
- Vegetable broth (for soups and stews)
- Lots of whole grains—rice, millet, barley, bulgur, quinoa, couscous, popcorn
- Pasta and noodles—Italian pasta, rice or quinoa noodles if you're gluten free, buckwheat soba. Almost all packaged pasta is vegan but fresh pasta is usually made with eggs.
- Whole-grain cereals and oatmeal (Steel-cut oats are best!)
- Peanut butter or almond butter
- Hummus
- Bread products—whole-grain bread (I like German black bread), tortillas, whole-grain pizza crusts
- Dried or canned beans—kidney, chickpeas, lentils, pintos, black, etc.

PRODUCE
- Fresh fruits and vegetables
- Frozen fruits and veggies
- Canned vegetables—artichokes, olives, tomatoes, hearts of palm, roasted red peppers
- Avocados

- Garlic and ginger, fresh or dried
- Lemons and limes (Unsweetened concentrate is good to have in the fridge to flavor water and homemade sodas.)

MEAT SUBSTITUTES
- Tofu, tempeh, seitan
- "Faux" meats, veggie burgers, soy hot dogs, burger crumbles, veggie sausage

DAIRY SWAPS
- Vegan butter (I like Earth Balance and Soy Garden.)
- Nondairy sour cream (I like Tofutti.)
- Egg replacement powder (Ener-G Egg Replacer), great for vegan baking
- Nondairy cream cheese (I like Kite Hill or Tofutti.)
- Nondairy cheese like nut cheese or soy-based cheeses (I like Daiya for pizza, Kite Hill for fancy, Follow Your Heart for whatevs.)
- Nondairy yogurt made with almond, soy, or coconut milk (Get the plain so it's not too sweet.)
- Nondairy frozen treats like ice cream made with coconut or soy milk, or chocolate-covered bananas (I'm looking at you, Trader Joe's!)

CONDIMENTS
- Soy sauce or tamari (gluten-free soy sauce)
- Vegan mayonnaise: Use in place of traditional mayonnaise in pasta and potato salads, sandwich spreads, and sauces; try Nayonaise or Vegenaise brands.
- Salsa, chutney, ketchup, mustard
- Vinegars, pickles, capers, chili paste, wasabi powder, Sriracha sauce

COOKING AIDS
- Oils—extra-virgin olive, dark sesame, coconut
- Tomato sauce: always useful in preparing last-minute meals
- Nutritional yeast: Use like grated Parm in breading, dressings, and soups as well as on pasta and popcorn.
- Agar: creates delicious vegan gelatin desserts and pudding
- Arrowroot and/or cornstarch: great as thickening agents in soups, stews, and sauces

SWEETENERS

- Pure maple syrup: an alternative to sugar for baking and for sauces
- Agave or brown rice syrup: can be used in place of honey in recipes
- Florida Crystals: unprocessed vegan sugar that can substitute for refined sugar in any recipe
- Coconut sugar
- Stevia (My fave. I like the liquid version in iced tea.)

ADDITIONAL HEALTHY STUFF

- Vegan protein powder
- Flax seeds, chia seeds

BULK FOODS (cheaper!)

- Dried fruits
- Dried mushrooms, dried chiles, sun-dried tomatoes
- Dried sea vegetables, including nori and agar
- Beans, nuts, seeds (flax, pumpkin, hemp, chia, sesame, sunflower)
- Whole grains and oats
- Nuts

RESOURCES

As you get more into the veganish lifestyle, you'll probably want to keep learning more about the subject. Here are some great resources:

ONLINE

Farm Sanctuary: www.farmsanctuary.org
The nation's largest farm animal rescue and protection organization and advocate of vegan education.

Forks Over Knives: www.forksoverknives.com
Recipes and information about plant-based diets.

Happy Cow: www.happycow.net
Vegan/vegetarian worldwide restaurant information guide.

Humane Society of the United States: www.humanesociety.org
An animal protection and education organization.

Mercy for Animals: www.mercyforanimals.org
An organization dedicated to preventing cruelty to farm animals and promoting compassionate food choices and policies.

The Post Punk Kitchen is my family's favorite place for recipes and tips. —Lydia, Hartland, ME

Mind Body Green: www.mindbodygreen.com
Website for environmentally friendly health information.

One Green Planet: www.onegreenplanet.org
An online guide to making conscious choices that help people, animals, and the planet.

> Watch the movie about how they make McDonald's food or watch Supersize Me. They really show you how unhealthy it is for you.
> —Miriam, Sacramento, CA

PETA: www.peta.org
People for the Ethical Treatment of Animals, an animal rights organization offering comprehensive vegan diet information.

peta2: www.peta2.com
This is the youth division of PETA.

Physicians Committee for Responsible Medicine: www.pcrm.org
An organization that promotes a vegan diet, preventive medicine, and alternatives to animal research.

Teens Turning Green: www.teensturninggreen.org

Teen Vegan: www.teenvgn.com

Vegetarian Resource Group: www.vrg.org
Vegetarian recipes and nutrition information dedicated to educating the public on vegetarianism and the interrelated issues of health, nutrition, ecology, and ethics.

VegYouth: www.vegyouth.com
And remember: If there's not a veganish group in your area, you can always start one!

APPS

American Farmers
A guide to locating farmers' markets across the U.S.

Animal Free
Information about hidden animal products found in foods. It also allows users to share hidden ingredients they know of or to review certain products. Includes a bar code scanner to check any product in its database.

Happy Cow
The website's guide to animal-free food, restaurants, and stores worldwide.

Is It Vegan?
Scan a product and find out if it's vegan.

Thrive Market
An online store for healthy-living products, and a great and cheap resource for nonperishable vegan food items (and other natural goods like beauty products).

VegOut
International listings of vegan, vegetarian, and vegetarian-friendly restaurants. Restaurant listings can be found by your exact location or a custom location if you're planning to travel.

Vegan Xpress
Lists vegan options available at a wide variety of mainstream restaurants, and animal product information about grocery items like alcohol, candy, and snacks.

Yelp
An online business directory that's not specifically vegan-related, but is an excellent aid for finding vegan restaurants, stores, and products.

BOOKS

- *Animal Liberation* by Peter Singer
- *Becoming Vegan* by Brenda Davis and Vesanto Melina, MD
- *Diet for a Small Planet* by Frances Moore Lappé
- *Dominion* by Matthew Scully
- *Dr. Neal Barnard's Program for Reversing Diabetes* by Neal Barnard, MD
- *Eating Animals* by Jonathan Safran Foer
- *Finding Ultra* by Rich Roll
- *How Not to Die* by Michael Greger, MD, and Gene Stone
- *The Blue Zones Solution* by Dan Buettner
- *The China Study* by Thomas Campbell and Dr. T. Colin Campbell
- *The Kind Diet* by Alicia Silverstone
- *The Pleasure Trap* by Douglas J. Lisle
- *The Starch Solution* by John McDougall, MD
- *Thrive* by Brendan Brazier
- *Yoga and Vegetarianism* by Sharon Gannon
- *The Lean* by yours truly. It's for someone who wants or needs to lose weight.

COOKBOOKS

- The many vegan cookbooks by the terrific chef who created the recipes in this book, Robin Robertson: *One Dish Vegan, Quick-Fix Vegan, Fresh from the Vegan Slow Cooker*
- *Afro-Vegan: Farm-Fresh African, Caribbean, and Southern Flavors Remixed* by Bryant Terry
- *Forks Over Knives* by Gene Stone, Dr. T. Colin Campbell, and Dr. Caldwell B. Esselstyn
- *Happy Healthy Vegan* by Kathy Patalsky
- *Isa Does It: Amazingly Easy, Wildly Delicious Vegan Recipes for Every Day of the Week* by Isa Chandra Moskowitz
- *The Conscious Cook: Delicious Meatless Recipes That Will Change the Way You Eat* by Tal Ronnen
- *The Joy of Vegan Baking* by Colleen Patrick-Goudreau
- *The Oh She Glows Cookbook* by Angela Liddon
- *The Vegan Stoner Cookbook: 100 Easy Vegan Recipes to Munch* by Sarah Conrique and Graham I. Haynes

- *Thug Kitchen* by Thug Kitchen
- *Vegan Lunch Box: 130 Amazing, Animal-free Lunches Kids and Grown-ups Will Love!* by Jennifer McCann
- *Veganomicon: The Ultimate Vegan Cookbook* by Isa Chandra Moskowitz and Terry Hope Romero

DOCUMENTARIES

- *Blackfish*
- *Cowspiracy*
- *Earthlings*
- *Fast Food Nation*
- *Fat, Sick and Nearly Dead*
- *Food Matters*
- *Food, Inc.*
- *Forks Over Knives*
- *Lunch Hour*
- *Racing Extinction*
- *Supersize Me*
- *The Cove*
- *Vegucated*

The experience that turned me vegetarian was watching the movie Temple Grandin. *Temple Grandin is an activist with autism who is an advocate for people with disabilities, and also for animal welfare. The movie explored her time working in a slaughterhouse. There is a scene where a cow is about to be slaughtered, and Temple puts her hand on its back to comfort it. Even though this movie was just a dramatization, you could still sense the fear and sadness in the cow's eyes. Then as the captive bolt is shoved into the cow's skull, its life vanishes, and it collapses on the ground. This scene forced me to confront the fact that meat was once a living, thinking, feeling creature, and that destroying sentient life just to satisfy a superficial palate preference is a tragedy.* —Danielle, Cincinnati, OH

ACKNOWLEDGMENTS

KATHY

A deep bow to the supersmart people who have been patient and forthcoming in addressing my relentless questions about health, ethics, environment, and psychology: you guys taught me how to drill down to the facts, to think things through, to question my manner of communication, and to keep my eye on the horizon. The message is so much stronger because of you: Neal Barnard, MD; Michael Greger, MD; Bruce Friedrich; Lisa Lange; Tal Ronnen; Melanie Joy, PhD. A big shout-out of appreciation to Ari Solomon for putting the word out to the many cool and articulate people who sent in their stories and testimonials. Thank you, too, to Robert Cheeke, for showing the path to a buff body!

The pages herein are so delicious because of the fabulous chef Robin Robertson, who jumped at the chance to write easy, practical recipes—she's not only incredibly talented, but also has a huge heart for people and animals. Thank you, Robin, for making this way of eating so infinitely doable!

Big love to Nicole Axworthy for shooting the awesome photos and making me jealous of her job (she got to eat everything after shooting it!). Thanks, lovely, artistic, kind lady!

A deep well of appreciation for Jennifer Rudolph Walsh at WME; you had the idea for this book, and you saw it through to fruition. Thank you, wise one!

So much gratitude goes to Pam Krauss for believing in and shepherding this book to publication, and for putting it in the übercapable, creative hands at Penguin Random House: Nina Caldas, Claire Vaccaro, Lauren Kolm, Meighan Cavanaugh, Tom Consiglio, Justin Thrift, and Claire Sullivan.

A celebratory toast to my very talented (and sassy) cowriter Rachel Cohn, who, from the moment I met her, exuded positivity and optimism. You made this project so fun, and you're a fantastic partner!

And to you, Dan Buettner, for listening, pushing, reading, exchanging, challenging, and growing with me. You are the best partner a gal could hope for.

RACHEL

Thanks to Team JRW; all the peer survey respondents (and outreach coordinators at MFA, PETA, and the Humane Society of the United States) for their generosity, enthusiasm, and great ideas; and deep nods of gratitude to Chloe Falkenheim and Chelsea Pula for their help and inspiration; and Ben Shaw, Miriam Silliman, and Natalie Silliman for being my awesome young veg guides.

Thank you to Pam Krauss and Nina Caldas for their superb editorial guidance, and much thanks to the amazing team at Avery Books/Penguin.

And a major thank-you to my vegan activist idol, Kathy. You inspire me, and one day I am going to fully break up with cheese. Thank you for lighting the way for anyone interested in "leaning in" to healthy, happy, ethical living. Much love and respect.

INDEX

Numbers in *italics* denote illustrations.

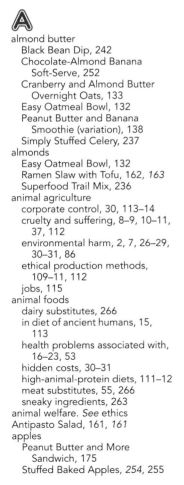

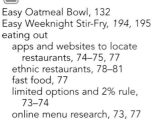